This Book Belongs To

Name: _____

Address: _____

Monthly Budget Overview

Income

Source	Budget	Actual
Main Income		
Extra Income		
Total Income		

Expences:

Category	Budget	Actual
Total		

Sinking funds

Source	Budget	Actual
Total		

Cash Envelopes:

Category	Budget	Actual
Total		

Total Cost to Withdraw: _____

Debt:

Source	Budget	Actual
Total		

Saving

Category	Add	Balance
Total		

	Budget	Actual
Total Funds:		

Monthly Budget Overview

Income

Source	Budget	Actual
Main Income		
Extra Income		
Total Income		

Expences:

Category	Budget	Actual
Total		

Sinking funds

Source	Budget	Actual
Total		

Cash Envelopes:

Category	Budget	Actual
Total		

Total Cost to Withdraw: _____

Debt:

Source	Budget	Actual
Total		

Saving

Category	Add	Balance
Total		

	Budget	Actual
Total Funds:		

Monthly Budget Overview

Income

Source	Budget	Actual
Main Income		
Extra Income		
Total Income		

Expences:

Category	Budget	Actual
Total		

Sinking funds

Source	Budget	Actual
Total		

Cash Envelopes:

Category	Budget	Actual
Total		

Total Cost to Withdraw: _____

Debt:

Source	Budget	Actual
Total		

Saving

Category	Add	Balance
Total		

	Budget	Actual
Total Funds:		

Monthly Budget Overview

Income

Source	Budget	Actual
Main Income		
Extra Income		
Total Income		

Expences:

Category	Budget	Actual
Total		

Sinking funds

Source	Budget	Actual
Total		

Cash Envelopes:

Category	Budget	Actual
Total		

Total Cost to Withdraw: _____

Debt:

Source	Budget	Actual
Total		

Saving

Category	Add	Balance
Total		

	Budget	Actual
Total Funds:		

Monthly Budget Overview

Income

Source	Budget	Actual
Main Income		
Extra Income		
Total Income		

Expences:

Category	Budget	Actual
Total		

Sinking funds

Source	Budget	Actual
Total		

Cash Envelopes:

Category	Budget	Actual
Total		

Total Cost to Withdraw: _____

Debt:

Source	Budget	Actual
Total		

Saving

Category	Add	Balance
Total		

	Budget	Actual
Total Funds:		

Monthly Budget Overview

Income

Source	Budget	Actual
Main Income		
Extra Income		
Total Income		

Expences:

Category	Budget	Actual
Total		

Sinking funds

Source	Budget	Actual
Total		

Cash Envelopes:

Category	Budget	Actual
Total		

Total Cost to Withdraw: _____

Debt:

Source	Budget	Actual
Total		

Saving

Category	Add	Balance
Total		

	Budget	Actual
Total Funds:		

Monthly Budget Overview

Income

Source	Budget	Actual
Main Income		
Extra Income		
Total Income		

Expences:

Category	Budget	Actual
Total		

Sinking funds

Source	Budget	Actual
Total		

Cash Envelopes:

Category	Budget	Actual
Total		

Total Cost to Withdraw: _____

Debt:

Source	Budget	Actual
Total		

Saving

Category	Add	Balance
Total		

	Budget	Actual
Total Funds:		

Monthly Budget Overview

Income

Source	Budget	Actual
Main Income		
Extra Income		
Total Income		

Expences:

Category	Budget	Actual
Total		

Sinking funds

Source	Budget	Actual
Total		

Cash Envelopes:

Category	Budget	Actual
Total		

Total Cost to Withdraw: _____

Debt:

Source	Budget	Actual
Total		

Saving

Category	Add	Balance
Total		

	Budget	Actual
Total Funds:		

Monthly Budget Overview

Income

Source	Budget	Actual
Main Income		
Extra Income		
Total Income		

Expences:

Category	Budget	Actual
Total		

Sinking funds

Source	Budget	Actual
Total		

Cash Envelopes:

Category	Budget	Actual
Total		

Total Cost to Withdraw: _____

Debt:

Source	Budget	Actual
Total		

Saving

Category	Add	Balance
Total		

	Budget	Actual
Total Funds:		

Monthly Budget Overview

Income

Source	Budget	Actual
Main Income		
Extra Income		
Total Income		

Expences:

Category	Budget	Actual
Total		

Sinking funds

Source	Budget	Actual
Total		

Cash Envelopes:

Category	Budget	Actual
Total		

Total Cost to Withdraw: _____

Debt:

Source	Budget	Actual
Total		

Saving

Category	Add	Balance
Total		

	Budget	Actual
Total Funds:		

Monthly Budget Overview

Income

Source	Budget	Actual
Main Income		
Extra Income		
Total Income		

Expences:

Category	Budget	Actual
Total		

Sinking funds

Source	Budget	Actual
Total		

Cash Envelopes:

Category	Budget	Actual
Total		

Total Cost to Withdraw: _____

Debt:

Source	Budget	Actual
Total		

Saving

Category	Add	Balance
Total		

	Budget	Actual
Total Funds:		

Monthly Budget Overview

Income

Source	Budget	Actual
Main Income		
Extra Income		
Total Income		

Expences:

Category	Budget	Actual
Total		

Sinking funds

Source	Budget	Actual
Total		

Cash Envelopes:

Category	Budget	Actual
Total		

Total Cost to Withdraw: _____

Debt:

Source	Budget	Actual
Total		

Saving

Category	Add	Balance
Total		

	Budget	Actual
Total Funds:		

Monthly Budget Overview

Income

Source	Budget	Actual
Main Income		
Extra Income		
Total Income		

Expences:

Category	Budget	Actual
Total		

Sinking funds

Source	Budget	Actual
Total		

Cash Envelopes:

Category	Budget	Actual
Total		

Total Cost to Withdraw: _____

Debt:

Source	Budget	Actual
Total		

Saving

Category	Add	Balance
Total		

	Budget	Actual
Total Funds:		

Monthly Budget Overview

Income

Source	Budget	Actual
Main Income		
Extra Income		
Total Income		

Expences:

Category	Budget	Actual
Total		

Sinking funds

Source	Budget	Actual
Total		

Cash Envelopes:

Category	Budget	Actual
Total		

Total Cost to Withdraw: _____

Debt:

Source	Budget	Actual
Total		

Saving

Category	Add	Balance
Total		

	Budget	Actual
Total Funds:		

Monthly Budget Overview

Income

Source	Budget	Actual
Main Income		
Extra Income		
Total Income		

Expences:

Category	Budget	Actual
Total		

Sinking funds

Source	Budget	Actual
Total		

Cash Envelopes:

Category	Budget	Actual
Total		

Total Cost to Withdraw: _____

Debt:

Source	Budget	Actual
Total		

Saving

Category	Add	Balance
Total		

	Budget	Actual
Total Funds:		

Monthly Budget Overview

Income

Source	Budget	Actual
Main Income		
Extra Income		
Total Income		

Expences:

Category	Budget	Actual
Total		

Sinking funds

Source	Budget	Actual
Total		

Cash Envelopes:

Category	Budget	Actual
Total		

Total Cost to Withdraw: _____

Debt:

Source	Budget	Actual
Total		

Saving

Category	Add	Balance
Total		

	Budget	Actual
Total Funds:		

Monthly Budget Overview

Income

Source	Budget	Actual
Main Income		
Extra Income		
Total Income		

Expences:

Category	Budget	Actual
Total		

Sinking funds

Source	Budget	Actual
Total		

Cash Envelopes:

Category	Budget	Actual
Total		

Total Cost to Withdraw: _____

Debt:

Source	Budget	Actual
Total		

Saving

Category	Add	Balance
Total		

	Budget	Actual
Total Funds:		

Monthly Budget Overview

Income

Source	Budget	Actual
Main Income		
Extra Income		
Total Income		

Expences:

Category	Budget	Actual
Total		

Sinking funds

Source	Budget	Actual
Total		

Cash Envelopes:

Category	Budget	Actual
Total		

Total Cost to Withdraw: _____

Debt:

Source	Budget	Actual
Total		

Saving

Category	Add	Balance
Total		

	Budget	Actual
Total Funds:		

Monthly Budget Overview

Income

Source	Budget	Actual
Main Income		
Extra Income		
Total Income		

Expences:

Category	Budget	Actual
Total		

Sinking funds

Source	Budget	Actual
Total		

Cash Envelopes:

Category	Budget	Actual
Total		

Total Cost to Withdraw: _____

Debt:

Source	Budget	Actual
Total		

Saving

Category	Add	Balance
Total		

	Budget	Actual
Total Funds:		

Monthly Budget Overview

Income

Source	Budget	Actual
Main Income		
Extra Income		
Total Income		

Expences:

Category	Budget	Actual
Total		

Sinking funds

Source	Budget	Actual
Total		

Cash Envelopes:

Category	Budget	Actual
Total		

Total Cost to Withdraw: _____

Debt:

Source	Budget	Actual
Total		

Saving

Category	Add	Balance
Total		

	Budget	Actual
Total Funds:		

Monthly Budget Overview

Income

Source	Budget	Actual
Main Income		
Extra Income		
Total Income		

Expences:

Category	Budget	Actual
Total		

Sinking funds

Source	Budget	Actual
Total		

Cash Envelopes:

Category	Budget	Actual
Total		

Total Cost to Withdraw: _____

Debt:

Source	Budget	Actual
Total		

Saving

Category	Add	Balance
Total		

	Budget	Actual
Total Funds:		

Monthly Budget Overview

Income

Source	Budget	Actual
Main Income		
Extra Income		
Total Income		

Expences:

Category	Budget	Actual
Total		

Sinking funds

Source	Budget	Actual
Total		

Cash Envelopes:

Category	Budget	Actual
Total		

Total Cost to Withdraw: _____

Debt:

Source	Budget	Actual
Total		

Saving

Category	Add	Balance
Total		

	Budget	Actual
Total Funds:		

Monthly Budget Overview

Income

Source	Budget	Actual
Main Income		
Extra Income		
Total Income		

Expences:

Category	Budget	Actual
Total		

Sinking funds

Source	Budget	Actual
Total		

Cash Envelopes:

Category	Budget	Actual
Total		

Total Cost to Withdraw: _____

Debt:

Source	Budget	Actual
Total		

Saving

Category	Add	Balance
Total		

	Budget	Actual
Total Funds:		

Monthly Budget Overview

Income

Source	Budget	Actual
Main Income		
Extra Income		
Total Income		

Expences:

Category	Budget	Actual
Total		

Sinking funds

Source	Budget	Actual
Total		

Cash Envelopes:

Category	Budget	Actual
Total		

Total Cost to Withdraw: _____

Debt:

Source	Budget	Actual
Total		

Saving

Category	Add	Balance
Total		

	Budget	Actual
Total Funds:		

Monthly Budget Overview

Income

Source	Budget	Actual
Main Income		
Extra Income		
Total Income		

Expences:

Category	Budget	Actual
Total		

Sinking funds

Source	Budget	Actual
Total		

Cash Envelopes:

Category	Budget	Actual
Total		

Total Cost to Withdraw: _____

Debt:

Source	Budget	Actual
Total		

Saving

Category	Add	Balance
Total		

	Budget	Actual
Total Funds:		

Monthly Budget Overview

Income

Source	Budget	Actual
Main Income		
Extra Income		
Total Income		

Expences:

Category	Budget	Actual
Total		

Sinking funds

Source	Budget	Actual
Total		

Cash Envelopes:

Category	Budget	Actual
Total		

Total Cost to Withdraw: _____

Debt:

Source	Budget	Actual
Total		

Saving

Category	Add	Balance
Total		

	Budget	Actual
Total Funds:		

Monthly Budget Overview

Income

Source	Budget	Actual
Main Income		
Extra Income		
Total Income		

Expences:

Category	Budget	Actual
Total		

Sinking funds

Source	Budget	Actual
Total		

Cash Envelopes:

Category	Budget	Actual
Total		

Total Cost to Withdraw: _____

Debt:

Source	Budget	Actual
Total		

Saving

Category	Add	Balance
Total		

	Budget	Actual
Total Funds:		

Monthly Budget Overview

Income

Source	Budget	Actual
Main Income		
Extra Income		
Total Income		

Expences:

Category	Budget	Actual
Total		

Sinking funds

Source	Budget	Actual
Total		

Cash Envelopes:

Category	Budget	Actual
Total		

Total Cost to Withdraw: _____

Debt:

Source	Budget	Actual
Total		

Saving

Category	Add	Balance
Total		

	Budget	Actual
Total Funds:		

Monthly Budget Overview

Income

Source	Budget	Actual
Main Income		
Extra Income		
Total Income		

Expences:

Category	Budget	Actual
Total		

Sinking funds

Source	Budget	Actual
Total		

Cash Envelopes:

Category	Budget	Actual
Total		

Total Cost to Withdraw: _____

Debt:

Source	Budget	Actual
Total		

Saving

Category	Add	Balance
Total		

	Budget	Actual
Total Funds:		

Monthly Budget Overview

Income

Source	Budget	Actual
Main Income		
Extra Income		
Total Income		

Expences:

Category	Budget	Actual
Total		

Sinking funds

Source	Budget	Actual
Total		

Cash Envelopes:

Category	Budget	Actual
Total		

Total Cost to Withdraw: _____

Debt:

Source	Budget	Actual
Total		

Saving

Category	Add	Balance
Total		

	Budget	Actual
Total Funds:		

Monthly Budget Overview

Income

Source	Budget	Actual
Main Income		
Extra Income		
Total Income		

Expences:

Category	Budget	Actual
Total		

Sinking funds

Source	Budget	Actual
Total		

Cash Envelopes:

Category	Budget	Actual
Total		

Total Cost to Withdraw: _____

Debt:

Source	Budget	Actual
Total		

Saving

Category	Add	Balance
Total		

	Budget	Actual
Total Funds:		

Monthly Budget Overview

Income

Source	Budget	Actual
Main Income		
Extra Income		
Total Income		

Expences:

Category	Budget	Actual
Total		

Sinking funds

Source	Budget	Actual
Total		

Cash Envelopes:

Category	Budget	Actual
Total		

Total Cost to Withdraw: _____

Debt:

Source	Budget	Actual
Total		

Saving

Category	Add	Balance
Total		

	Budget	Actual
Total Funds:		

Monthly Budget Overview

Income

Source	Budget	Actual
Main Income		
Extra Income		
Total Income		

Expences:

Category	Budget	Actual
Total		

Sinking funds

Source	Budget	Actual
Total		

Cash Envelopes:

Category	Budget	Actual
Total		

Total Cost to Withdraw: _____

Debt:

Source	Budget	Actual
Total		

Saving

Category	Add	Balance
Total		

	Budget	Actual
Total Funds:		

Monthly Budget Overview

Income

Source	Budget	Actual
Main Income		
Extra Income		
Total Income		

Expences:

Category	Budget	Actual
Total		

Sinking funds

Source	Budget	Actual
Total		

Cash Envelopes:

Category	Budget	Actual
Total		

Total Cost to Withdraw: _____

Debt:

Source	Budget	Actual
Total		

Saving

Category	Add	Balance
Total		

	Budget	Actual
Total Funds:		

Monthly Budget Overview

Income

Source	Budget	Actual
Main Income		
Extra Income		
Total Income		

Expences:

Category	Budget	Actual
Total		

Sinking funds

Source	Budget	Actual
Total		

Cash Envelopes:

Category	Budget	Actual
Total		

Total Cost to Withdraw: _____

Debt:

Source	Budget	Actual
Total		

Saving

Category	Add	Balance
Total		

	Budget	Actual
Total Funds:		

Monthly Budget Overview

Income

Source	Budget	Actual
Main Income		
Extra Income		
Total Income		

Expences:

Category	Budget	Actual
Total		

Sinking funds

Source	Budget	Actual
Total		

Cash Envelopes:

Category	Budget	Actual
Total		

Total Cost to Withdraw: _____

Debt:

Source	Budget	Actual
Total		

Saving

Category	Add	Balance
Total		

	Budget	Actual
Total Funds:		

Monthly Budget Overview

Income

Source	Budget	Actual
Main Income		
Extra Income		
Total Income		

Expences:

Category	Budget	Actual
Total		

Sinking funds

Source	Budget	Actual
Total		

Cash Envelopes:

Category	Budget	Actual
Total		

Total Cost to Withdraw: _____

Debt:

Source	Budget	Actual
Total		

Saving

Category	Add	Balance
Total		

	Budget	Actual
Total Funds:		

Monthly Budget Overview

Income

Source	Budget	Actual
Main Income		
Extra Income		
Total Income		

Expences:

Category	Budget	Actual
Total		

Sinking funds

Source	Budget	Actual
Total		

Cash Envelopes:

Category	Budget	Actual
Total		

Total Cost to Withdraw: _____

Debt:

Source	Budget	Actual
Total		

Saving

Category	Add	Balance
Total		

	Budget	Actual
Total Funds:		

Monthly Budget Overview

Income

Source	Budget	Actual
Main Income		
Extra Income		
Total Income		

Expences:

Category	Budget	Actual
Total		

Sinking funds

Source	Budget	Actual
Total		

Cash Envelopes:

Category	Budget	Actual
Total		

Total Cost to Withdraw: _____

Debt:

Source	Budget	Actual
Total		

Saving

Category	Add	Balance
Total		

	Budget	Actual
Total Funds:		

Monthly Budget Overview

Income

Source	Budget	Actual
Main Income		
Extra Income		
Total Income		

Expences:

Category	Budget	Actual
Total		

Sinking funds

Source	Budget	Actual
Total		

Cash Envelopes:

Category	Budget	Actual
Total		

Total Cost to Withdraw: _____

Debt:

Source	Budget	Actual
Total		

Saving

Category	Add	Balance
Total		

	Budget	Actual
Total Funds:		

Monthly Budget Overview

Income

Source	Budget	Actual
Main Income		
Extra Income		
Total Income		

Expences:

Category	Budget	Actual
Total		

Sinking funds

Source	Budget	Actual
Total		

Cash Envelopes:

Category	Budget	Actual
Total		

Total Cost to Withdraw: _____

Debt:

Source	Budget	Actual
Total		

Saving

Category	Add	Balance
Total		

	Budget	Actual
Total Funds:		

Monthly Budget Overview

Income

Source	Budget	Actual
Main Income		
Extra Income		
Total Income		

Expences:

Category	Budget	Actual
Total		

Sinking funds

Source	Budget	Actual
Total		

Cash Envelopes:

Category	Budget	Actual
Total		

Total Cost to Withdraw: _____

Debt:

Source	Budget	Actual
Total		

Saving

Category	Add	Balance
Total		

	Budget	Actual
Total Funds:		

Monthly Budget Overview

Income

Source	Budget	Actual
Main Income		
Extra Income		
Total Income		

Expences:

Category	Budget	Actual
Total		

Sinking funds

Source	Budget	Actual
Total		

Cash Envelopes:

Category	Budget	Actual
Total		

Total Cost to Withdraw: _____

Debt:

Source	Budget	Actual
Total		

Saving

Category	Add	Balance
Total		

	Budget	Actual
Total Funds:		

Monthly Budget Overview

Income

Source	Budget	Actual
Main Income		
Extra Income		
Total Income		

Expences:

Category	Budget	Actual
Total		

Sinking funds

Source	Budget	Actual
Total		

Cash Envelopes:

Category	Budget	Actual
Total		

Total Cost to Withdraw: _____

Debt:

Source	Budget	Actual
Total		

Saving

Category	Add	Balance
Total		

	Budget	Actual
Total Funds:		

Monthly Budget Overview

Income

Source	Budget	Actual
Main Income		
Extra Income		
Total Income		

Expences:

Category	Budget	Actual
Total		

Sinking funds

Source	Budget	Actual
Total		

Cash Envelopes:

Category	Budget	Actual
Total		

Total Cost to Withdraw: _____

Debt:

Source	Budget	Actual
Total		

Saving

Category	Add	Balance
Total		

	Budget	Actual
Total Funds:		

Monthly Budget Overview

Income

Source	Budget	Actual
Main Income		
Extra Income		
Total Income		

Expences:

Category	Budget	Actual
Total		

Sinking funds

Source	Budget	Actual
Total		

Cash Envelopes:

Category	Budget	Actual
Total		

Total Cost to Withdraw: _____

Debt:

Source	Budget	Actual
Total		

Saving

Category	Add	Balance
Total		

	Budget	Actual
Total Funds:		

Monthly Budget Overview

Income

Source	Budget	Actual
Main Income		
Extra Income		
Total Income		

Expences:

Category	Budget	Actual
Total		

Sinking funds

Source	Budget	Actual
Total		

Cash Envelopes:

Category	Budget	Actual
Total		

Total Cost to Withdraw: _____

Debt:

Source	Budget	Actual
Total		

Saving

Category	Add	Balance
Total		

	Budget	Actual
Total Funds:		

Monthly Budget Overview

Income

Source	Budget	Actual
Main Income		
Extra Income		
Total Income		

Expences:

Category	Budget	Actual
Total		

Sinking funds

Source	Budget	Actual
Total		

Cash Envelopes:

Category	Budget	Actual
Total		

Total Cost to Withdraw: _____

Debt:

Source	Budget	Actual
Total		

Saving

Category	Add	Balance
Total		

	Budget	Actual
Total Funds:		

Monthly Budget Overview

Income

Source	Budget	Actual
Main Income		
Extra Income		
Total Income		

Expences:

Category	Budget	Actual
Total		

Sinking funds

Source	Budget	Actual
Total		

Cash Envelopes:

Category	Budget	Actual
Total		

Debt:

Source	Budget	Actual
Total		

Saving

Category	Add	Balance
Total		

Total Cost to Withdraw: _____

	Budget	Actual
Total Funds:		

Monthly Budget Overview

Income

Source	Budget	Actual
Main Income		
Extra Income		
Total Income		

Expences:

Category	Budget	Actual
Total		

Sinking funds

Source	Budget	Actual
Total		

Cash Envelopes:

Category	Budget	Actual
Total		

Total Cost to Withdraw: _____

Debt:

Source	Budget	Actual
Total		

Saving

Category	Add	Balance
Total		

	Budget	Actual
Total Funds:		

Monthly Budget Overview

Income

Source	Budget	Actual
Main Income		
Extra Income		
Total Income		

Expences:

Category	Budget	Actual
Total		

Sinking funds

Source	Budget	Actual
Total		

Cash Envelopes:

Category	Budget	Actual
Total		

Total Cost to Withdraw: _____

Debt:

Source	Budget	Actual
Total		

Saving

Category	Add	Balance
Total		

	Budget	Actual
Total Funds:		

Monthly Budget Overview

Income

Source	Budget	Actual
Main Income		
Extra Income		
Total Income		

Expences:

Category	Budget	Actual
Total		

Sinking funds

Source	Budget	Actual
Total		

Cash Envelopes:

Category	Budget	Actual
Total		

Total Cost to Withdraw: _____

Debt:

Source	Budget	Actual
Total		

Saving

Category	Add	Balance
Total		

	Budget	Actual
Total Funds:		

Monthly Budget Overview

Income

Source	Budget	Actual
Main Income		
Extra Income		
Total Income		

Expences:

Category	Budget	Actual
Total		

Sinking funds

Source	Budget	Actual
Total		

Cash Envelopes:

Category	Budget	Actual
Total		

Total Cost to Withdraw: _____

Debt:

Source	Budget	Actual
Total		

Saving

Category	Add	Balance
Total		

	Budget	Actual
Total Funds:		

Monthly Budget Overview

Income

Source	Budget	Actual
Main Income		
Extra Income		
Total Income		

Expences:

Category	Budget	Actual
Total		

Sinking funds

Source	Budget	Actual
Total		

Cash Envelopes:

Category	Budget	Actual
Total		

Total Cost to Withdraw: _____

Debt:

Source	Budget	Actual
Total		

Saving

Category	Add	Balance
Total		

	Budget	Actual
Total Funds:		

Monthly Budget Overview

Income

Source	Budget	Actual
Main Income		
Extra Income		
Total Income		

Expences:

Category	Budget	Actual
Total		

Sinking funds

Source	Budget	Actual
Total		

Cash Envelopes:

Category	Budget	Actual
Total		

Total Cost to Withdraw: _____

Debt:

Source	Budget	Actual
Total		

Saving

Category	Add	Balance
Total		

	Budget	Actual
Total Funds:		

Monthly Budget Overview

Income

Source	Budget	Actual
Main Income		
Extra Income		
Total Income		

Expences:

Category	Budget	Actual
Total		

Sinking funds

Source	Budget	Actual
Total		

Cash Envelopes:

Category	Budget	Actual
Total		

Total Cost to Withdraw: _____

Debt:

Source	Budget	Actual
Total		

Saving

Category	Add	Balance
Total		

	Budget	Actual
Total Funds:		

Monthly Budget Overview

Income

Source	Budget	Actual
Main Income		
Extra Income		
Total Income		

Expences:

Category	Budget	Actual
Total		

Sinking funds

Source	Budget	Actual
Total		

Cash Envelopes:

Category	Budget	Actual
Total		

Total Cost to Withdraw: _____

Debt:

Source	Budget	Actual
Total		

Saving

Category	Add	Balance
Total		

	Budget	Actual
Total Funds:		

Monthly Budget Overview

Income

Source	Budget	Actual
Main Income		
Extra Income		
Total Income		

Expences:

Category	Budget	Actual
Total		

Sinking funds

Source	Budget	Actual
Total		

Cash Envelopes:

Category	Budget	Actual
Total		

Total Cost to Withdraw: _____

Debt:

Source	Budget	Actual
Total		

Saving

Category	Add	Balance
Total		

	Budget	Actual
Total Funds:		

Monthly Budget Overview

Income

Source	Budget	Actual
Main Income		
Extra Income		
Total Income		

Expences:

Category	Budget	Actual
Total		

Sinking funds

Source	Budget	Actual
Total		

Cash Envelopes:

Category	Budget	Actual
Total		

Total Cost to Withdraw: _____

Debt:

Source	Budget	Actual
Total		

Saving

Category	Add	Balance
Total		

	Budget	Actual
Total Funds:		

Monthly Budget Overview

Income

Source	Budget	Actual
Main Income		
Extra Income		
Total Income		

Expences:

Category	Budget	Actual
Total		

Sinking funds

Source	Budget	Actual
Total		

Cash Envelopes:

Category	Budget	Actual
Total		

Total Cost to Withdraw: _____

Debt:

Source	Budget	Actual
Total		

Saving

Category	Add	Balance
Total		

	Budget	Actual
Total Funds:		

Monthly Budget Overview

Income

Source	Budget	Actual
Main Income		
Extra Income		
Total Income		

Expences:

Category	Budget	Actual
Total		

Sinking funds

Source	Budget	Actual
Total		

Cash Envelopes:

Category	Budget	Actual
Total		

Total Cost to Withdraw: _____

Debt:

Source	Budget	Actual
Total		

Saving

Category	Add	Balance
Total		

	Budget	Actual
Total Funds:		

Monthly Budget Overview

Income

Source	Budget	Actual
Main Income		
Extra Income		
Total Income		

Expences:

Category	Budget	Actual
Total		

Sinking funds

Source	Budget	Actual
Total		

Cash Envelopes:

Category	Budget	Actual
Total		

Total Cost to Withdraw: _____

Debt:

Source	Budget	Actual
Total		

Saving

Category	Add	Balance
Total		

	Budget	Actual
Total Funds:		

Monthly Budget Overview

Income

Source	Budget	Actual
Main Income		
Extra Income		
Total Income		

Expences:

Category	Budget	Actual
Total		

Sinking funds

Source	Budget	Actual
Total		

Cash Envelopes:

Category	Budget	Actual
Total		

Total Cost to Withdraw: _____

Debt:

Source	Budget	Actual
Total		

Saving

Category	Add	Balance
Total		

	Budget	Actual
Total Funds:		

Monthly Budget Overview

Income

Source	Budget	Actual
Main Income		
Extra Income		
Total Income		

Expences:

Category	Budget	Actual
Total		

Sinking funds

Source	Budget	Actual
Total		

Cash Envelopes:

Category	Budget	Actual
Total		

Total Cost to Withdraw: _____

Debt:

Source	Budget	Actual
Total		

Saving

Category	Add	Balance
Total		

	Budget	Actual
Total Funds:		

Monthly Budget Overview

Income

Source	Budget	Actual
Main Income		
Extra Income		
Total Income		

Expences:

Category	Budget	Actual
Total		

Sinking funds

Source	Budget	Actual
Total		

Cash Envelopes:

Category	Budget	Actual
Total		

Total Cost to Withdraw: _____

Debt:

Source	Budget	Actual
Total		

Saving

Category	Add	Balance
Total		

	Budget	Actual
Total Funds:		

Monthly Budget Overview

Income

Source	Budget	Actual
Main Income		
Extra Income		
Total Income		

Expences:

Category	Budget	Actual
Total		

Sinking funds

Source	Budget	Actual
Total		

Cash Envelopes:

Category	Budget	Actual
Total		

Total Cost to Withdraw: _____

Debt:

Source	Budget	Actual
Total		

Saving

Category	Add	Balance
Total		

	Budget	Actual
Total Funds:		

Monthly Budget Overview

Income

Source	Budget	Actual
Main Income		
Extra Income		
Total Income		

Expences:

Category	Budget	Actual
Total		

Sinking funds

Source	Budget	Actual
Total		

Cash Envelopes:

Category	Budget	Actual
Total		

Total Cost to Withdraw: _____

Debt:

Source	Budget	Actual
Total		

Saving

Category	Add	Balance
Total		

	Budget	Actual
Total Funds:		

Monthly Budget Overview

Income

Source	Budget	Actual
Main Income		
Extra Income		
Total Income		

Expences:

Category	Budget	Actual
Total		

Sinking funds

Source	Budget	Actual
Total		

Cash Envelopes:

Category	Budget	Actual
Total		

Total Cost to Withdraw: _____

Debt:

Source	Budget	Actual
Total		

Saving

Category	Add	Balance
Total		

	Budget	Actual
Total Funds:		

Monthly Budget Overview

Income

Source	Budget	Actual
Main Income		
Extra Income		
Total Income		

Expences:

Category	Budget	Actual
Total		

Sinking funds

Source	Budget	Actual
Total		

Cash Envelopes:

Category	Budget	Actual
Total		

Total Cost to Withdraw: _____

Debt:

Source	Budget	Actual
Total		

Saving

Category	Add	Balance
Total		

	Budget	Actual
Total Funds:		

Monthly Budget Overview

Income

Source	Budget	Actual
Main Income		
Extra Income		
Total Income		

Expences:

Category	Budget	Actual
Total		

Sinking funds

Source	Budget	Actual
Total		

Cash Envelopes:

Category	Budget	Actual
Total		

Total Cost to Withdraw: _____

Debt:

Source	Budget	Actual
Total		

Saving

Category	Add	Balance
Total		

	Budget	Actual
Total Funds:		

Monthly Budget Overview

Income

Source	Budget	Actual
Main Income		
Extra Income		
Total Income		

Expences:

Category	Budget	Actual
Total		

Sinking funds

Source	Budget	Actual
Total		

Cash Envelopes:

Category	Budget	Actual
Total		

Total Cost to Withdraw: _____

Debt:

Source	Budget	Actual
Total		

Saving

Category	Add	Balance
Total		

	Budget	Actual
Total Funds:		

Monthly Budget Overview

Income

Source	Budget	Actual
Main Income		
Extra Income		
Total Income		

Expences:

Category	Budget	Actual
Total		

Sinking funds

Source	Budget	Actual
Total		

Cash Envelopes:

Category	Budget	Actual
Total		

Total Cost to Withdraw: _____

Debt:

Source	Budget	Actual
Total		

Saving

Category	Add	Balance
Total		

	Budget	Actual
Total Funds:		

Monthly Budget Overview

Income

Source	Budget	Actual
Main Income		
Extra Income		
Total Income		

Expences:

Category	Budget	Actual
Total		

Sinking funds

Source	Budget	Actual
Total		

Cash Envelopes:

Category	Budget	Actual
Total		

Total Cost to Withdraw: _____

Debt:

Source	Budget	Actual
Total		

Saving

Category	Add	Balance
Total		

	Budget	Actual
Total Funds:		

Monthly Budget Overview

Income

Source	Budget	Actual
Main Income		
Extra Income		
Total Income		

Expences:

Category	Budget	Actual
Total		

Sinking funds

Source	Budget	Actual
Total		

Cash Envelopes:

Category	Budget	Actual
Total		

Total Cost to Withdraw: _____

Debt:

Source	Budget	Actual
Total		

Saving

Category	Add	Balance
Total		

	Budget	Actual
Total Funds:		

Monthly Budget Overview

Income

Source	Budget	Actual
Main Income		
Extra Income		
Total Income		

Expences:

Category	Budget	Actual
Total		

Sinking funds

Source	Budget	Actual
Total		

Cash Envelopes:

Category	Budget	Actual
Total		

Total Cost to Withdraw: _____

Debt:

Source	Budget	Actual
Total		

Saving

Category	Add	Balance
Total		

	Budget	Actual
Total Funds:		

Monthly Budget Overview

Income

Source	Budget	Actual
Main Income		
Extra Income		
Total Income		

Expences:

Category	Budget	Actual
Total		

Sinking funds

Source	Budget	Actual
Total		

Cash Envelopes:

Category	Budget	Actual
Total		

Total Cost to Withdraw: _____

Debt:

Source	Budget	Actual
Total		

Saving

Category	Add	Balance
Total		

	Budget	Actual
Total Funds:		

Monthly Budget Overview

Income

Source	Budget	Actual
Main Income		
Extra Income		
Total Income		

Expences:

Category	Budget	Actual
Total		

Sinking funds

Source	Budget	Actual
Total		

Cash Envelopes:

Category	Budget	Actual
Total		

Total Cost to Withdraw: _____

Debt:

Source	Budget	Actual
Total		

Saving

Category	Add	Balance
Total		

	Budget	Actual
Total Funds:		

Monthly Budget Overview

Income

Source	Budget	Actual
Main Income		
Extra Income		
Total Income		

Expences:

Category	Budget	Actual
Total		

Sinking funds

Source	Budget	Actual
Total		

Cash Envelopes:

Category	Budget	Actual
Total		

Total Cost to Withdraw: _____

Debt:

Source	Budget	Actual
Total		

Saving

Category	Add	Balance
Total		

	Budget	Actual
Total Funds:		

Monthly Budget Overview

Income

Source	Budget	Actual
Main Income		
Extra Income		
Total Income		

Expences:

Category	Budget	Actual
Total		

Sinking funds

Source	Budget	Actual
Total		

Cash Envelopes:

Category	Budget	Actual
Total		

Total Cost to Withdraw: _____

Debt:

Source	Budget	Actual
Total		

Saving

Category	Add	Balance
Total		

	Budget	Actual
Total Funds:		

Monthly Budget Overview

Income

Source	Budget	Actual
Main Income		
Extra Income		
Total Income		

Expences:

Category	Budget	Actual
Total		

Sinking funds

Source	Budget	Actual
Total		

Cash Envelopes:

Category	Budget	Actual
Total		

Total Cost to Withdraw: _____

Debt:

Source	Budget	Actual
Total		

Saving

Category	Add	Balance
Total		

	Budget	Actual
Total Funds:		

Monthly Budget Overview

Income

Source	Budget	Actual
Main Income		
Extra Income		
Total Income		

Expences:

Category	Budget	Actual
Total		

Sinking funds

Source	Budget	Actual
Total		

Cash Envelopes:

Category	Budget	Actual
Total		

Total Cost to Withdraw: _____

Debt:

Source	Budget	Actual
Total		

Saving

Category	Add	Balance
Total		

	Budget	Actual
Total Funds:		

Monthly Budget Overview

Income

Source	Budget	Actual
Main Income		
Extra Income		
Total Income		

Expences:

Category	Budget	Actual
Total		

Sinking funds

Source	Budget	Actual
Total		

Cash Envelopes:

Category	Budget	Actual
Total		

Total Cost to Withdraw: _____

Debt:

Source	Budget	Actual
Total		

Saving

Category	Add	Balance
Total		

	Budget	Actual
Total Funds:		

Monthly Budget Overview

Income

Source	Budget	Actual
Main Income		
Extra Income		
Total Income		

Expences:

Category	Budget	Actual
Total		

Sinking funds

Source	Budget	Actual
Total		

Cash Envelopes:

Category	Budget	Actual
Total		

Total Cost to Withdraw: _____

Debt:

Source	Budget	Actual
Total		

Saving

Category	Add	Balance
Total		

	Budget	Actual
Total Funds:		

Monthly Budget Overview

Income

Source	Budget	Actual
Main Income		
Extra Income		
Total Income		

Expences:

Category	Budget	Actual
Total		

Sinking funds

Source	Budget	Actual
Total		

Cash Envelopes:

Category	Budget	Actual
Total		

Total Cost to Withdraw: _____

Debt:

Source	Budget	Actual
Total		

Saving

Category	Add	Balance
Total		

	Budget	Actual
Total Funds:		

Monthly Budget Overview

Income

Source	Budget	Actual
Main Income		
Extra Income		
Total Income		

Expences:

Category	Budget	Actual
Total		

Sinking funds

Source	Budget	Actual
Total		

Cash Envelopes:

Category	Budget	Actual
Total		

Total Cost to Withdraw: _____

Debt:

Source	Budget	Actual
Total		

Saving

Category	Add	Balance
Total		

	Budget	Actual
Total Funds:		

Monthly Budget Overview

Income

Source	Budget	Actual
Main Income		
Extra Income		
Total Income		

Expences:

Category	Budget	Actual
Total		

Sinking funds

Source	Budget	Actual
Total		

Cash Envelopes:

Category	Budget	Actual
Total		

Total Cost to Withdraw: _____

Debt:

Source	Budget	Actual
Total		

Saving

Category	Add	Balance
Total		

	Budget	Actual
Total Funds:		

Monthly Budget Overview

Income

Source	Budget	Actual
Main Income		
Extra Income		
Total Income		

Expences:

Category	Budget	Actual
Total		

Sinking funds

Source	Budget	Actual
Total		

Cash Envelopes:

Category	Budget	Actual
Total		

Total Cost to Withdraw: _____

Debt:

Source	Budget	Actual
Total		

Saving

Category	Add	Balance
Total		

	Budget	Actual
Total Funds:		

Monthly Budget Overview

Income

Source	Budget	Actual
Main Income		
Extra Income		
Total Income		

Expences:

Category	Budget	Actual
Total		

Sinking funds

Source	Budget	Actual
Total		

Cash Envelopes:

Category	Budget	Actual
Total		

Total Cost to Withdraw: _____

Debt:

Source	Budget	Actual
Total		

Saving

Category	Add	Balance
Total		

	Budget	Actual
Total Funds:		

Monthly Budget Overview

Income

Source	Budget	Actual
Main Income		
Extra Income		
Total Income		

Expences:

Category	Budget	Actual
Total		

Sinking funds

Source	Budget	Actual
Total		

Cash Envelopes:

Category	Budget	Actual
Total		

Total Cost to Withdraw: _____

Debt:

Source	Budget	Actual
Total		

Saving

Category	Add	Balance
Total		

	Budget	Actual
Total Funds:		

Monthly Budget Overview

Income

Source	Budget	Actual
Main Income		
Extra Income		
Total Income		

Expences:

Category	Budget	Actual
Total		

Sinking funds

Source	Budget	Actual
Total		

Cash Envelopes:

Category	Budget	Actual
Total		

Total Cost to Withdraw: _____

Debt:

Source	Budget	Actual
Total		

Saving

Category	Add	Balance
Total		

	Budget	Actual
Total Funds:		

Monthly Budget Overview

Income

Source	Budget	Actual
Main Income		
Extra Income		
Total Income		

Expences:

Category	Budget	Actual
Total		

Sinking funds

Source	Budget	Actual
Total		

Cash Envelopes:

Category	Budget	Actual
Total		

Debt:

Source	Budget	Actual
Total		

Saving

Category	Add	Balance
Total		

	Budget	Actual
Total Funds:		

Total Cost to Withdraw: _____

Monthly Budget Overview

Income

Source	Budget	Actual
Main Income		
Extra Income		
Total Income		

Expences:

Category	Budget	Actual
Total		

Sinking funds

Source	Budget	Actual
Total		

Cash Envelopes:

Category	Budget	Actual
Total		

Total Cost to Withdraw: _____

Debt:

Source	Budget	Actual
Total		

Saving

Category	Add	Balance
Total		

	Budget	Actual
Total Funds:		

Monthly Budget Overview

Income

Source	Budget	Actual
Main Income		
Extra Income		
Total Income		

Expences:

Category	Budget	Actual
Total		

Sinking funds

Source	Budget	Actual
Total		

Cash Envelopes:

Category	Budget	Actual
Total		

Total Cost to Withdraw: _____

Debt:

Source	Budget	Actual
Total		

Saving

Category	Add	Balance
Total		

	Budget	Actual
Total Funds:		

Monthly Budget Overview

Income

Source	Budget	Actual
Main Income		
Extra Income		
Total Income		

Expences:

Category	Budget	Actual
Total		

Sinking funds

Source	Budget	Actual
Total		

Cash Envelopes:

Category	Budget	Actual
Total		

Total Cost to Withdraw: _____

Debt:

Source	Budget	Actual
Total		

Saving

Category	Add	Balance
Total		

	Budget	Actual
Total Funds:		

Monthly Budget Overview

Income

Source	Budget	Actual
Main Income		
Extra Income		
Total Income		

Expences:

Category	Budget	Actual
Total		

Sinking funds

Source	Budget	Actual
Total		

Cash Envelopes:

Category	Budget	Actual
Total		

Total Cost to Withdraw: _____

Debt:

Source	Budget	Actual
Total		

Saving

Category	Add	Balance
Total		

	Budget	Actual
Total Funds:		

Monthly Budget Overview

Income

Source	Budget	Actual
Main Income		
Extra Income		
Total Income		

Expences:

Category	Budget	Actual
Total		

Sinking funds

Source	Budget	Actual
Total		

Cash Envelopes:

Category	Budget	Actual
Total		

Total Cost to Withdraw: _____

Debt:

Source	Budget	Actual
Total		

Saving

Category	Add	Balance
Total		

	Budget	Actual
Total Funds:		

Monthly Budget Overview

Income

Source	Budget	Actual
Main Income		
Extra Income		
Total Income		

Expences:

Category	Budget	Actual
Total		

Sinking funds

Source	Budget	Actual
Total		

Cash Envelopes:

Category	Budget	Actual
Total		

Total Cost to Withdraw: _____

Debt:

Source	Budget	Actual
Total		

Saving

Category	Add	Balance
Total		

	Budget	Actual
Total Funds:		

Monthly Budget Overview

Income

Source	Budget	Actual
Main Income		
Extra Income		
Total Income		

Expences:

Category	Budget	Actual
Total		

Sinking funds

Source	Budget	Actual
Total		

Cash Envelopes:

Category	Budget	Actual
Total		

Total Cost to Withdraw: _____

Debt:

Source	Budget	Actual
Total		

Saving

Category	Add	Balance
Total		

	Budget	Actual
Total Funds:		

Monthly Budget Overview

Income

Source	Budget	Actual
Main Income		
Extra Income		
Total Income		

Expences:

Category	Budget	Actual
Total		

Sinking funds

Source	Budget	Actual
Total		

Cash Envelopes:

Category	Budget	Actual
Total		

Total Cost to Withdraw: _____

Debt:

Source	Budget	Actual
Total		

Saving

Category	Add	Balance
Total		

	Budget	Actual
Total Funds:		

Monthly Budget Overview

Income

Source	Budget	Actual
Main Income		
Extra Income		
Total Income		

Expences:

Category	Budget	Actual
Total		

Sinking funds

Source	Budget	Actual
Total		

Cash Envelopes:

Category	Budget	Actual
Total		

Total Cost to Withdraw: _____

Debt:

Source	Budget	Actual
Total		

Saving

Category	Add	Balance
Total		

	Budget	Actual
Total Funds:		

Monthly Budget Overview

Income

Source	Budget	Actual
Main Income		
Extra Income		
Total Income		

Expences:

Category	Budget	Actual
Total		

Sinking funds

Source	Budget	Actual
Total		

Cash Envelopes:

Category	Budget	Actual
Total		

Debt:

Source	Budget	Actual
Total		

Saving

Category	Add	Balance
Total		

Total Cost to Withdraw: _____

	Budget	Actual
Total Funds:		

Monthly Budget Overview

Income

Source	Budget	Actual
Main Income		
Extra Income		
Total Income		

Expences:

Category	Budget	Actual
Total		

Sinking funds

Source	Budget	Actual
Total		

Cash Envelopes:

Category	Budget	Actual
Total		

Total Cost to Withdraw: _____

Debt:

Source	Budget	Actual
Total		

Saving

Category	Add	Balance
Total		

	Budget	Actual
Total Funds:		

Monthly Budget Overview

Income

Source	Budget	Actual
Main Income		
Extra Income		
Total Income		

Expences:

Category	Budget	Actual
Total		

Sinking funds

Source	Budget	Actual
Total		

Cash Envelopes:

Category	Budget	Actual
Total		

Debt:

Source	Budget	Actual
Total		

Saving

Category	Add	Balance
Total		

Total Cost to Withdraw: _____

	Budget	Actual
Total Funds:		

Monthly Budget Overview

Income

Source	Budget	Actual
Main Income		
Extra Income		
Total Income		

Expences:

Category	Budget	Actual
Total		

Sinking funds

Source	Budget	Actual
Total		

Cash Envelopes:

Category	Budget	Actual
Total		

Total Cost to Withdraw: _____

Debt:

Source	Budget	Actual
Total		

Saving

Category	Add	Balance
Total		

	Budget	Actual
Total Funds:		

Monthly Budget Overview

Income

Source	Budget	Actual
Main Income		
Extra Income		
Total Income		

Expences:

Category	Budget	Actual
Total		

Sinking funds

Source	Budget	Actual
Total		

Cash Envelopes:

Category	Budget	Actual
Total		

Total Cost to Withdraw: _____

Debt:

Source	Budget	Actual
Total		

Saving

Category	Add	Balance
Total		

	Budget	Actual
Total Funds:		

Monthly Budget Overview

Income

Source	Budget	Actual
Main Income		
Extra Income		
Total Income		

Expences:

Category	Budget	Actual
Total		

Sinking funds

Source	Budget	Actual
Total		

Cash Envelopes:

Category	Budget	Actual
Total		

Total Cost to Withdraw: _____

Debt:

Source	Budget	Actual
Total		

Saving

Category	Add	Balance
Total		

	Budget	Actual
Total Funds:		

Monthly Budget Overview

Income

Source	Budget	Actual
Main Income		
Extra Income		
Total Income		

Expences:

Category	Budget	Actual
Total		

Sinking funds

Source	Budget	Actual
Total		

Cash Envelopes:

Category	Budget	Actual
Total		

Total Cost to Withdraw: _____

Debt:

Source	Budget	Actual
Total		

Saving

Category	Add	Balance
Total		

	Budget	Actual
Total Funds:		

Monthly Budget Overview

Income

Source	Budget	Actual
Main Income		
Extra Income		
Total Income		

Expences:

Category	Budget	Actual
Total		

Sinking funds

Source	Budget	Actual
Total		

Cash Envelopes:

Category	Budget	Actual
Total		

Total Cost to Withdraw: _____

Debt:

Source	Budget	Actual
Total		

Saving

Category	Add	Balance
Total		

	Budget	Actual
Total Funds:		

Monthly Budget Overview

Income

Source	Budget	Actual
Main Income		
Extra Income		
Total Income		

Expences:

Category	Budget	Actual
Total		

Sinking funds

Source	Budget	Actual
Total		

Cash Envelopes:

Category	Budget	Actual
Total		

Debt:

Source	Budget	Actual
Total		

Saving

Category	Add	Balance
Total		

Total Cost to Withdraw: _____

	Budget	Actual
Total Funds:		

Monthly Budget Overview

Income

Source	Budget	Actual
Main Income		
Extra Income		
Total Income		

Expences:

Category	Budget	Actual
Total		

Sinking funds

Source	Budget	Actual
Total		

Cash Envelopes:

Category	Budget	Actual
Total		

Total Cost to Withdraw: _____

Debt:

Source	Budget	Actual
Total		

Saving

Category	Add	Balance
Total		

	Budget	Actual
Total Funds:		

Monthly Budget Overview

Income

Source	Budget	Actual
Main Income		
Extra Income		
Total Income		

Expences:

Category	Budget	Actual
Total		

Sinking funds

Source	Budget	Actual
Total		

Cash Envelopes:

Category	Budget	Actual
Total		

Total Cost to Withdraw: _____

Debt:

Source	Budget	Actual
Total		

Saving

Category	Add	Balance
Total		

	Budget	Actual
Total Funds:		

Monthly Budget Overview

Income

Source	Budget	Actual
Main Income		
Extra Income		
Total Income		

Expences:

Category	Budget	Actual
Total		

Sinking funds

Source	Budget	Actual
Total		

Cash Envelopes:

Category	Budget	Actual
Total		

Total Cost to Withdraw: _____

Debt:

Source	Budget	Actual
Total		

Saving

Category	Add	Balance
Total		

	Budget	Actual
Total Funds:		

Monthly Budget Overview

Income

Source	Budget	Actual
Main Income		
Extra Income		
Total Income		

Expences:

Category	Budget	Actual
Total		

Sinking funds

Source	Budget	Actual
Total		

Cash Envelopes:

Category	Budget	Actual
Total		

Total Cost to Withdraw: _____

Debt:

Source	Budget	Actual
Total		

Saving

Category	Add	Balance
Total		

	Budget	Actual
Total Funds:		

Monthly Budget Overview

Income

Source	Budget	Actual
Main Income		
Extra Income		
Total Income		

Expences:

Category	Budget	Actual
Total		

Sinking funds

Source	Budget	Actual
Total		

Cash Envelopes:

Category	Budget	Actual
Total		

Total Cost to Withdraw: _____

Debt:

Source	Budget	Actual
Total		

Saving

Category	Add	Balance
Total		

	Budget	Actual
Total Funds:		

Monthly Budget Overview

Income

Source	Budget	Actual
Main Income		
Extra Income		
Total Income		

Expences:

Category	Budget	Actual
Total		

Sinking funds

Source	Budget	Actual
Total		

Cash Envelopes:

Category	Budget	Actual
Total		

Total Cost to Withdraw: _____

Debt:

Source	Budget	Actual
Total		

Saving

Category	Add	Balance
Total		

	Budget	Actual
Total Funds:		

Monthly Budget Overview

Income

Source	Budget	Actual
Main Income		
Extra Income		
Total Income		

Expences:

Category	Budget	Actual
Total		

Sinking funds

Source	Budget	Actual
Total		

Cash Envelopes:

Category	Budget	Actual
Total		

Total Cost to Withdraw: _____

Debt:

Source	Budget	Actual
Total		

Saving

Category	Add	Balance
Total		

	Budget	Actual
Total Funds:		

Monthly Budget Overview

Income

Source	Budget	Actual
Main Income		
Extra Income		
Total Income		

Expences:

Category	Budget	Actual
Total		

Sinking funds

Source	Budget	Actual
Total		

Cash Envelopes:

Category	Budget	Actual
Total		

Total Cost to Withdraw: _____

Debt:

Source	Budget	Actual
Total		

Saving

Category	Add	Balance
Total		

	Budget	Actual
Total Funds:		

Monthly Budget Overview

Income

Source	Budget	Actual
Main Income		
Extra Income		
Total Income		

Expences:

Category	Budget	Actual
Total		

Sinking funds

Source	Budget	Actual
Total		

Cash Envelopes:

Category	Budget	Actual
Total		

Total Cost to Withdraw: _____

Debt:

Source	Budget	Actual
Total		

Saving

Category	Add	Balance
Total		

	Budget	Actual
Total Funds:		

Monthly Budget Overview

Income

Source	Budget	Actual
Main Income		
Extra Income		
Total Income		

Expences:

Category	Budget	Actual
Total		

Sinking funds

Source	Budget	Actual
Total		

Cash Envelopes:

Category	Budget	Actual
Total		

Total Cost to Withdraw: _____

Debt:

Source	Budget	Actual
Total		

Saving

Category	Add	Balance
Total		

	Budget	Actual
Total Funds:		

Monthly Budget Overview

Income

Source	Budget	Actual
Main Income		
Extra Income		
Total Income		

Expences:

Category	Budget	Actual
Total		

Sinking funds

Source	Budget	Actual
Total		

Cash Envelopes:

Category	Budget	Actual
Total		

Total Cost to Withdraw: _____

Debt:

Source	Budget	Actual
Total		

Saving

Category	Add	Balance
Total		

	Budget	Actual
Total Funds:		

Monthly Budget Overview

Income

Source	Budget	Actual
Main Income		
Extra Income		
Total Income		

Expences:

Category	Budget	Actual
Total		

Sinking funds

Source	Budget	Actual
Total		

Cash Envelopes:

Category	Budget	Actual
Total		

Total Cost to Withdraw: _____

Debt:

Source	Budget	Actual
Total		

Saving

Category	Add	Balance
Total		

	Budget	Actual
Total Funds:		

Monthly Budget Overview

Income

Source	Budget	Actual
Main Income		
Extra Income		
Total Income		

Expences:

Category	Budget	Actual
Total		

Sinking funds

Source	Budget	Actual
Total		

Cash Envelopes:

Category	Budget	Actual
Total		

Total Cost to Withdraw: _____

Debt:

Source	Budget	Actual
Total		

Saving

Category	Add	Balance
Total		

	Budget	Actual
Total Funds:		

Monthly Budget Overview

Income

Source	Budget	Actual
Main Income		
Extra Income		
Total Income		

Expences:

Category	Budget	Actual
Total		

Sinking funds

Source	Budget	Actual
Total		

Cash Envelopes:

Category	Budget	Actual
Total		

Total Cost to Withdraw: _____

Debt:

Source	Budget	Actual
Total		

Saving

Category	Add	Balance
Total		

	Budget	Actual
Total Funds:		

Monthly Budget Overview

Income

Source	Budget	Actual
Main Income		
Extra Income		
Total Income		

Expences:

Category	Budget	Actual
Total		

Sinking funds

Source	Budget	Actual
Total		

Cash Envelopes:

Category	Budget	Actual
Total		

Total Cost to Withdraw: _____

Debt:

Source	Budget	Actual
Total		

Saving

Category	Add	Balance
Total		

	Budget	Actual
Total Funds:		

Monthly Budget Overview

Income

Source	Budget	Actual
Main Income		
Extra Income		
Total Income		

Expences:

Category	Budget	Actual
Total		

Sinking funds

Source	Budget	Actual
Total		

Cash Envelopes:

Category	Budget	Actual
Total		

Total Cost to Withdraw: _____

Debt:

Source	Budget	Actual
Total		

Saving

Category	Add	Balance
Total		

	Budget	Actual
Total Funds:		

Monthly Budget Overview

Income

Source	Budget	Actual
Main Income		
Extra Income		
Total Income		

Expences:

Category	Budget	Actual
Total		

Sinking funds

Source	Budget	Actual
Total		

Cash Envelopes:

Category	Budget	Actual
Total		

Total Cost to Withdraw: _____

Debt:

Source	Budget	Actual
Total		

Saving

Category	Add	Balance
Total		

	Budget	Actual
Total Funds:		

Monthly Budget Overview

Income

Source	Budget	Actual
Main Income		
Extra Income		
Total Income		

Expences:

Category	Budget	Actual
Total		

Sinking funds

Source	Budget	Actual
Total		

Cash Envelopes:

Category	Budget	Actual
Total		

Total Cost to Withdraw: _____

Debt:

Source	Budget	Actual
Total		

Saving

Category	Add	Balance
Total		

	Budget	Actual
Total Funds:		

Monthly Budget Overview

Income

Source	Budget	Actual
Main Income		
Extra Income		
Total Income		

Expences:

Category	Budget	Actual
Total		

Sinking funds

Source	Budget	Actual
Total		

Cash Envelopes:

Category	Budget	Actual
Total		

Total Cost to Withdraw: _____

Debt:

Source	Budget	Actual
Total		

Saving

Category	Add	Balance
Total		

	Budget	Actual
Total Funds:		

Monthly Budget Overview

Income

Source	Budget	Actual
Main Income		
Extra Income		
Total Income		

Expences:

Category	Budget	Actual
Total		

Sinking funds

Source	Budget	Actual
Total		

Cash Envelopes:

Category	Budget	Actual
Total		

Total Cost to Withdraw: _____

Debt:

Source	Budget	Actual
Total		

Saving

Category	Add	Balance
Total		

	Budget	Actual
Total Funds:		

Monthly Budget Overview

Income

Source	Budget	Actual
Main Income		
Extra Income		
Total Income		

Expences:

Category	Budget	Actual
Total		

Sinking funds

Source	Budget	Actual
Total		

Cash Envelopes:

Category	Budget	Actual
Total		

Total Cost to Withdraw: _____

Debt:

Source	Budget	Actual
Total		

Saving

Category	Add	Balance
Total		

	Budget	Actual
Total Funds:		

Monthly Budget Overview

Income

Source	Budget	Actual
Main Income		
Extra Income		
Total Income		

Expences:

Category	Budget	Actual
Total		

Sinking funds

Source	Budget	Actual
Total		

Cash Envelopes:

Category	Budget	Actual
Total		

Total Cost to Withdraw: _____

Debt:

Source	Budget	Actual
Total		

Saving

Category	Add	Balance
Total		

	Budget	Actual
Total Funds:		

Monthly Budget Overview

Income

Source	Budget	Actual
Main Income		
Extra Income		
Total Income		

Expences:

Category	Budget	Actual
Total		

Sinking funds

Source	Budget	Actual
Total		

Cash Envelopes:

Category	Budget	Actual
Total		

Total Cost to Withdraw: _____

Debt:

Source	Budget	Actual
Total		

Saving

Category	Add	Balance
Total		

	Budget	Actual
Total Funds:		

Monthly Budget Overview

Income

Source	Budget	Actual
Main Income		
Extra Income		
Total Income		

Expences:

Category	Budget	Actual
Total		

Sinking funds

Source	Budget	Actual
Total		

Cash Envelopes:

Category	Budget	Actual
Total		

Total Cost to Withdraw: _____

Debt:

Source	Budget	Actual
Total		

Saving

Category	Add	Balance
Total		

	Budget	Actual
Total Funds:		

Monthly Budget Overview

Income

Source	Budget	Actual
Main Income		
Extra Income		
Total Income		

Expences:

Category	Budget	Actual
Total		

Sinking funds

Source	Budget	Actual
Total		

Cash Envelopes:

Category	Budget	Actual
Total		

Total Cost to Withdraw: _____

Debt:

Source	Budget	Actual
Total		

Saving

Category	Add	Balance
Total		

	Budget	Actual
Total Funds:		

Monthly Budget Overview

Income

Source	Budget	Actual
Main Income		
Extra Income		
Total Income		

Expences:

Category	Budget	Actual
Total		

Sinking funds

Source	Budget	Actual
Total		

Cash Envelopes:

Category	Budget	Actual
Total		

Total Cost to Withdraw: _____

Debt:

Source	Budget	Actual
Total		

Saving

Category	Add	Balance
Total		

	Budget	Actual
Total Funds:		

Monthly Budget Overview

Income

Source	Budget	Actual
Main Income		
Extra Income		
Total Income		

Expences:

Category	Budget	Actual
Total		

Sinking funds

Source	Budget	Actual
Total		

Cash Envelopes:

Category	Budget	Actual
Total		

Total Cost to Withdraw: _____

Debt:

Source	Budget	Actual
Total		

Saving

Category	Add	Balance
Total		

	Budget	Actual
Total Funds:		

Monthly Budget Overview

Income

Source	Budget	Actual
Main Income		
Extra Income		
Total Income		

Expences:

Category	Budget	Actual
Total		

Sinking funds

Source	Budget	Actual
Total		

Cash Envelopes:

Category	Budget	Actual
Total		

Total Cost to Withdraw: _____

Debt:

Source	Budget	Actual
Total		

Saving

Category	Add	Balance
Total		

	Budget	Actual
Total Funds:		

Monthly Budget Overview

Income

Source	Budget	Actual
Main Income		
Extra Income		
Total Income		

Expences:

Category	Budget	Actual
Total		

Sinking funds

Source	Budget	Actual
Total		

Cash Envelopes:

Category	Budget	Actual
Total		

Total Cost to Withdraw: _____

Debt:

Source	Budget	Actual
Total		

Saving

Category	Add	Balance
Total		

	Budget	Actual
Total Funds:		

Monthly Budget Overview

Income

Source	Budget	Actual
Main Income		
Extra Income		
Total Income		

Expences:

Category	Budget	Actual
Total		

Sinking funds

Source	Budget	Actual
Total		

Cash Envelopes:

Category	Budget	Actual
Total		

Debt:

Source	Budget	Actual
Total		

Saving

Category	Add	Balance
Total		

Total Cost to Withdraw: _____

	Budget	Actual
Total Funds:		

Monthly Budget Overview

Income

Source	Budget	Actual
Main Income		
Extra Income		
Total Income		

Expences:

Category	Budget	Actual
Total		

Sinking funds

Source	Budget	Actual
Total		

Cash Envelopes:

Category	Budget	Actual
Total		

Total Cost to Withdraw: _____

Debt:

Source	Budget	Actual
Total		

Saving

Category	Add	Balance
Total		

	Budget	Actual
Total Funds:		

Monthly Budget Overview

Income

Source	Budget	Actual
Main Income		
Extra Income		
Total Income		

Expences:

Category	Budget	Actual
Total		

Sinking funds

Source	Budget	Actual
Total		

Cash Envelopes:

Category	Budget	Actual
Total		

Total Cost to Withdraw: _____

Debt:

Source	Budget	Actual
Total		

Saving

Category	Add	Balance
Total		

	Budget	Actual
Total Funds:		

Monthly Budget Overview

Income

Source	Budget	Actual
Main Income		
Extra Income		
Total Income		

Expences:

Category	Budget	Actual
Total		

Sinking funds

Source	Budget	Actual
Total		

Cash Envelopes:

Category	Budget	Actual
Total		

Total Cost to Withdraw: _____

Debt:

Source	Budget	Actual
Total		

Saving

Category	Add	Balance
Total		

	Budget	Actual
Total Funds:		

Monthly Budget Overview

Income

Source	Budget	Actual
Main Income		
Extra Income		
Total Income		

Expences:

Category	Budget	Actual
Total		

Sinking funds

Source	Budget	Actual
Total		

Cash Envelopes:

Category	Budget	Actual
Total		

Total Cost to Withdraw: _____

Debt:

Source	Budget	Actual
Total		

Saving

Category	Add	Balance
Total		

	Budget	Actual
Total Funds:		

Monthly Budget Overview

Income

Source	Budget	Actual
Main Income		
Extra Income		
Total Income		

Expences:

Category	Budget	Actual
Total		

Sinking funds

Source	Budget	Actual
Total		

Cash Envelopes:

Category	Budget	Actual
Total		

Total Cost to Withdraw: _____

Debt:

Source	Budget	Actual
Total		

Saving

Category	Add	Balance
Total		

	Budget	Actual
Total Funds:		

Monthly Budget Overview

Income

Source	Budget	Actual
Main Income		
Extra Income		
Total Income		

Expences:

Category	Budget	Actual
Total		

Sinking funds

Source	Budget	Actual
Total		

Cash Envelopes:

Category	Budget	Actual
Total		

Total Cost to Withdraw: _____

Debt:

Source	Budget	Actual
Total		

Saving

Category	Add	Balance
Total		

	Budget	Actual
Total Funds:		

Monthly Budget Overview

Income

Source	Budget	Actual
Main Income		
Extra Income		
Total Income		

Expences:

Category	Budget	Actual
Total		

Sinking funds

Source	Budget	Actual
Total		

Cash Envelopes:

Category	Budget	Actual
Total		

Total Cost to Withdraw: _____

Debt:

Source	Budget	Actual
Total		

Saving

Category	Add	Balance
Total		

	Budget	Actual
Total Funds:		

Monthly Budget Overview

Income

Source	Budget	Actual
Main Income		
Extra Income		
Total Income		

Expences:

Category	Budget	Actual
Total		

Sinking funds

Source	Budget	Actual
Total		

Cash Envelopes:

Category	Budget	Actual
Total		

Total Cost to Withdraw: _____

Debt:

Source	Budget	Actual
Total		

Saving

Category	Add	Balance
Total		

	Budget	Actual
Total Funds:		

Monthly Budget Overview

Income

Source	Budget	Actual
Main Income		
Extra Income		
Total Income		

Expences:

Category	Budget	Actual
Total		

Sinking funds

Source	Budget	Actual
Total		

Cash Envelopes:

Category	Budget	Actual
Total		

Total Cost to Withdraw: _____

Debt:

Source	Budget	Actual
Total		

Saving

Category	Add	Balance
Total		

	Budget	Actual
Total Funds:		

Monthly Budget Overview

Income

Source	Budget	Actual
Main Income		
Extra Income		
Total Income		

Expences:

Category	Budget	Actual
Total		

Sinking funds

Source	Budget	Actual
Total		

Cash Envelopes:

Category	Budget	Actual
Total		

Total Cost to Withdraw: _____

Debt:

Source	Budget	Actual
Total		

Saving

Category	Add	Balance
Total		

	Budget	Actual
Total Funds:		

Monthly Budget Overview

Income

Source	Budget	Actual
Main Income		
Extra Income		
Total Income		

Expences:

Category	Budget	Actual
Total		

Sinking funds

Source	Budget	Actual
Total		

Cash Envelopes:

Category	Budget	Actual
Total		

Total Cost to Withdraw: _____

Debt:

Source	Budget	Actual
Total		

Saving

Category	Add	Balance
Total		

	Budget	Actual
Total Funds:		

Monthly Budget Overview

Income

Source	Budget	Actual
Main Income		
Extra Income		
Total Income		

Expences:

Category	Budget	Actual
Total		

Sinking funds

Source	Budget	Actual
Total		

Cash Envelopes:

Category	Budget	Actual
Total		

Total Cost to Withdraw: _____

Debt:

Source	Budget	Actual
Total		

Saving

Category	Add	Balance
Total		

	Budget	Actual
Total Funds:		

Monthly Budget Overview

Income

Source	Budget	Actual
Main Income		
Extra Income		
Total Income		

Expences:

Category	Budget	Actual
Total		

Sinking funds

Source	Budget	Actual
Total		

Cash Envelopes:

Category	Budget	Actual
Total		

Total Cost to Withdraw: _____

Debt:

Source	Budget	Actual
Total		

Saving

Category	Add	Balance
Total		

	Budget	Actual
Total Funds:		

Monthly Budget Overview

Income

Source	Budget	Actual
Main Income		
Extra Income		
Total Income		

Expences:

Category	Budget	Actual
Total		

Sinking funds

Source	Budget	Actual
Total		

Cash Envelopes:

Category	Budget	Actual
Total		

Total Cost to Withdraw: _____

Debt:

Source	Budget	Actual
Total		

Saving

Category	Add	Balance
Total		

	Budget	Actual
Total Funds:		

Monthly Budget Overview

Income

Source	Budget	Actual
Main Income		
Extra Income		
Total Income		

Expences:

Category	Budget	Actual
Total		

Sinking funds

Source	Budget	Actual
Total		

Cash Envelopes:

Category	Budget	Actual
Total		

Total Cost to Withdraw: _____

Debt:

Source	Budget	Actual
Total		

Saving

Category	Add	Balance
Total		

	Budget	Actual
Total Funds:		

Monthly Budget Overview

Income

Source	Budget	Actual
Main Income		
Extra Income		
Total Income		

Expences:

Category	Budget	Actual
Total		

Sinking funds

Source	Budget	Actual
Total		

Cash Envelopes:

Category	Budget	Actual
Total		

Total Cost to Withdraw: _____

Debt:

Source	Budget	Actual
Total		

Saving

Category	Add	Balance
Total		

	Budget	Actual
Total Funds:		

Monthly Budget Overview

Income

Source	Budget	Actual
Main Income		
Extra Income		
Total Income		

Expences:

Category	Budget	Actual
Total		

Sinking funds

Source	Budget	Actual
Total		

Cash Envelopes:

Category	Budget	Actual
Total		

Total Cost to Withdraw: _____

Debt:

Source	Budget	Actual
Total		

Saving

Category	Add	Balance
Total		

	Budget	Actual
Total Funds:		

Monthly Budget Overview

Income

Source	Budget	Actual
Main Income		
Extra Income		
Total Income		

Expences:

Category	Budget	Actual
Total		

Sinking funds

Source	Budget	Actual
Total		

Cash Envelopes:

Category	Budget	Actual
Total		

Total Cost to Withdraw: _____

Debt:

Source	Budget	Actual
Total		

Saving

Category	Add	Balance
Total		

	Budget	Actual
Total Funds:		

Monthly Budget Overview

Income

Source	Budget	Actual
Main Income		
Extra Income		
Total Income		

Expences:

Category	Budget	Actual
Total		

Sinking funds

Source	Budget	Actual
Total		

Cash Envelopes:

Category	Budget	Actual
Total		

Total Cost to Withdraw: _____

Debt:

Source	Budget	Actual
Total		

Saving

Category	Add	Balance
Total		

	Budget	Actual
Total Funds:		

Monthly Budget Overview

Income

Source	Budget	Actual
Main Income		
Extra Income		
Total Income		

Expences:

Category	Budget	Actual
Total		

Sinking funds

Source	Budget	Actual
Total		

Cash Envelopes:

Category	Budget	Actual
Total		

Total Cost to Withdraw: _____

Debt:

Source	Budget	Actual
Total		

Saving

Category	Add	Balance
Total		

	Budget	Actual
Total Funds:		

Monthly Budget Overview

Income

Source	Budget	Actual
Main Income		
Extra Income		
Total Income		

Expences:

Category	Budget	Actual
Total		

Sinking funds

Source	Budget	Actual
Total		

Cash Envelopes:

Category	Budget	Actual
Total		

Total Cost to Withdraw: _____

Debt:

Source	Budget	Actual
Total		

Saving

Category	Add	Balance
Total		

	Budget	Actual
Total Funds:		

Monthly Budget Overview

Income

Source	Budget	Actual
Main Income		
Extra Income		
Total Income		

Expences:

Category	Budget	Actual
Total		

Sinking funds

Source	Budget	Actual
Total		

Cash Envelopes:

Category	Budget	Actual
Total		

Total Cost to Withdraw: _____

Debt:

Source	Budget	Actual
Total		

Saving

Category	Add	Balance
Total		

	Budget	Actual
Total Funds:		

Monthly Budget Overview

Income

Source	Budget	Actual
Main Income		
Extra Income		
Total Income		

Expences:

Category	Budget	Actual
Total		

Sinking funds

Source	Budget	Actual
Total		

Cash Envelopes:

Category	Budget	Actual
Total		

Total Cost to Withdraw: _____

Debt:

Source	Budget	Actual
Total		

Saving

Category	Add	Balance
Total		

	Budget	Actual
Total Funds:		

Monthly Budget Overview

Income

Source	Budget	Actual
Main Income		
Extra Income		
Total Income		

Expences:

Category	Budget	Actual
Total		

Sinking funds

Source	Budget	Actual
Total		

Cash Envelopes:

Category	Budget	Actual
Total		

Total Cost to Withdraw: _____

Debt:

Source	Budget	Actual
Total		

Saving

Category	Add	Balance
Total		

	Budget	Actual
Total Funds:		

Monthly Budget Overview

Income

Source	Budget	Actual
Main Income		
Extra Income		
Total Income		

Expences:

Category	Budget	Actual
Total		

Sinking funds

Source	Budget	Actual
Total		

Cash Envelopes:

Category	Budget	Actual
Total		

Total Cost to Withdraw: _____

Debt:

Source	Budget	Actual
Total		

Saving

Category	Add	Balance
Total		

	Budget	Actual
Total Funds:		

Monthly Budget Overview

Income

Source	Budget	Actual
Main Income		
Extra Income		
Total Income		

Expences:

Category	Budget	Actual
Total		

Sinking funds

Source	Budget	Actual
Total		

Cash Envelopes:

Category	Budget	Actual
Total		

Total Cost to Withdraw: _____

Debt:

Source	Budget	Actual
Total		

Saving

Category	Add	Balance
Total		

	Budget	Actual
Total Funds:		

Monthly Budget Overview

Income

Source	Budget	Actual
Main Income		
Extra Income		
Total Income		

Expences:

Category	Budget	Actual
Total		

Sinking funds

Source	Budget	Actual
Total		

Cash Envelopes:

Category	Budget	Actual
Total		

Total Cost to Withdraw: _____

Debt:

Source	Budget	Actual
Total		

Saving

Category	Add	Balance
Total		

	Budget	Actual
Total Funds:		

Monthly Budget Overview

Income

Source	Budget	Actual
Main Income		
Extra Income		
Total Income		

Expences:

Category	Budget	Actual
Total		

Sinking funds

Source	Budget	Actual
Total		

Cash Envelopes:

Category	Budget	Actual
Total		

Total Cost to Withdraw: _____

Debt:

Source	Budget	Actual
Total		

Saving

Category	Add	Balance
Total		

	Budget	Actual
Total Funds:		

Monthly Budget Overview

Income

Source	Budget	Actual
Main Income		
Extra Income		
Total Income		

Expences:

Category	Budget	Actual
Total		

Sinking funds

Source	Budget	Actual
Total		

Cash Envelopes:

Category	Budget	Actual
Total		

Total Cost to Withdraw: _____

Debt:

Source	Budget	Actual
Total		

Saving

Category	Add	Balance
Total		

	Budget	Actual
Total Funds:		

Monthly Budget Overview

Income

Source	Budget	Actual
Main Income		
Extra Income		
Total Income		

Expences:

Category	Budget	Actual
Total		

Sinking funds

Source	Budget	Actual
Total		

Cash Envelopes:

Category	Budget	Actual
Total		

Total Cost to Withdraw: _____

Debt:

Source	Budget	Actual
Total		

Saving

Category	Add	Balance
Total		

	Budget	Actual
Total Funds:		

Monthly Budget Overview

Income

Source	Budget	Actual
Main Income		
Extra Income		
Total Income		

Expences:

Category	Budget	Actual
Total		

Sinking funds

Source	Budget	Actual
Total		

Cash Envelopes:

Category	Budget	Actual
Total		

Total Cost to Withdraw: _____

Debt:

Source	Budget	Actual
Total		

Saving

Category	Add	Balance
Total		

	Budget	Actual
Total Funds:		

Monthly Budget Overview

Income

Source	Budget	Actual
Main Income		
Extra Income		
Total Income		

Expences:

Category	Budget	Actual
Total		

Sinking funds

Source	Budget	Actual
Total		

Cash Envelopes:

Category	Budget	Actual
Total		

Total Cost to Withdraw: _____

Debt:

Source	Budget	Actual
Total		

Saving

Category	Add	Balance
Total		

	Budget	Actual
Total Funds:		

Monthly Budget Overview

Income

Source	Budget	Actual
Main Income		
Extra Income		
Total Income		

Expences:

Category	Budget	Actual
Total		

Sinking funds

Source	Budget	Actual
Total		

Cash Envelopes:

Category	Budget	Actual
Total		

Total Cost to Withdraw: _____

Debt:

Source	Budget	Actual
Total		

Saving

Category	Add	Balance
Total		

	Budget	Actual
Total Funds:		

Monthly Budget Overview

Income

Source	Budget	Actual
Main Income		
Extra Income		
Total Income		

Expences:

Category	Budget	Actual
Total		

Sinking funds

Source	Budget	Actual
Total		

Cash Envelopes:

Category	Budget	Actual
Total		

Total Cost to Withdraw: _____

Debt:

Source	Budget	Actual
Total		

Saving

Category	Add	Balance
Total		

	Budget	Actual
Total Funds:		

Monthly Budget Overview

Income

Source	Budget	Actual
Main Income		
Extra Income		
Total Income		

Expences:

Category	Budget	Actual
Total		

Sinking funds

Source	Budget	Actual
Total		

Cash Envelopes:

Category	Budget	Actual
Total		

Total Cost to Withdraw: _____

Debt:

Source	Budget	Actual
Total		

Saving

Category	Add	Balance
Total		

	Budget	Actual
Total Funds:		

Monthly Budget Overview

Income

Source	Budget	Actual
Main Income		
Extra Income		
Total Income		

Expences:

Category	Budget	Actual
Total		

Sinking funds

Source	Budget	Actual
Total		

Cash Envelopes:

Category	Budget	Actual
Total		

Total Cost to Withdraw: _____

Debt:

Source	Budget	Actual
Total		

Saving

Category	Add	Balance
Total		

	Budget	Actual
Total Funds:		

Monthly Budget Overview

Income

Source	Budget	Actual
Main Income		
Extra Income		
Total Income		

Expences:

Category	Budget	Actual
Total		

Sinking funds

Source	Budget	Actual
Total		

Cash Envelopes:

Category	Budget	Actual
Total		

Total Cost to Withdraw: _____

Debt:

Source	Budget	Actual
Total		

Saving

Category	Add	Balance
Total		

	Budget	Actual
Total Funds:		

Monthly Budget Overview

Income

Source	Budget	Actual
Main Income		
Extra Income		
Total Income		

Expences:

Category	Budget	Actual
Total		

Sinking funds

Source	Budget	Actual
Total		

Cash Envelopes:

Category	Budget	Actual
Total		

Total Cost to Withdraw: _____

Debt:

Source	Budget	Actual
Total		

Saving

Category	Add	Balance
Total		

	Budget	Actual
Total Funds:		

Monthly Budget Overview

Income

Source	Budget	Actual
Main Income		
Extra Income		
Total Income		

Expences:

Category	Budget	Actual
Total		

Sinking funds

Source	Budget	Actual
Total		

Cash Envelopes:

Category	Budget	Actual
Total		

Total Cost to Withdraw: _____

Debt:

Source	Budget	Actual
Total		

Saving

Category	Add	Balance
Total		

	Budget	Actual
Total Funds:		

Monthly Budget Overview

Income

Source	Budget	Actual
Main Income		
Extra Income		
Total Income		

Expences:

Category	Budget	Actual
Total		

Sinking funds

Source	Budget	Actual
Total		

Cash Envelopes:

Category	Budget	Actual
Total		

Total Cost to Withdraw: _____

Debt:

Source	Budget	Actual
Total		

Saving

Category	Add	Balance
Total		

	Budget	Actual
Total Funds:		

Monthly Budget Overview

Income

Source	Budget	Actual
Main Income		
Extra Income		
Total Income		

Expences:

Category	Budget	Actual
Total		

Sinking funds

Source	Budget	Actual
Total		

Cash Envelopes:

Category	Budget	Actual
Total		

Total Cost to Withdraw: _____

Debt:

Source	Budget	Actual
Total		

Saving

Category	Add	Balance
Total		

	Budget	Actual
Total Funds:		

Monthly Budget Overview

Income

Source	Budget	Actual
Main Income		
Extra Income		
Total Income		

Expences:

Category	Budget	Actual
Total		

Sinking funds

Source	Budget	Actual
Total		

Cash Envelopes:

Category	Budget	Actual
Total		

Debt:

Source	Budget	Actual
Total		

Saving

Category	Add	Balance
Total		

Total Cost to Withdraw: _____

	Budget	Actual
Total Funds:		

Monthly Budget Overview

Income

Source	Budget	Actual
Main Income		
Extra Income		
Total Income		

Expences:

Category	Budget	Actual
Total		

Sinking funds

Source	Budget	Actual
Total		

Cash Envelopes:

Category	Budget	Actual
Total		

Total Cost to Withdraw: _____

Debt:

Source	Budget	Actual
Total		

Saving

Category	Add	Balance
Total		

	Budget	Actual
Total Funds:		

Monthly Budget Overview

Income

Source	Budget	Actual
Main Income		
Extra Income		
Total Income		

Expences:

Category	Budget	Actual
Total		

Sinking funds

Source	Budget	Actual
Total		

Cash Envelopes:

Category	Budget	Actual
Total		

Total Cost to Withdraw: _____

Debt:

Source	Budget	Actual
Total		

Saving

Category	Add	Balance
Total		

	Budget	Actual
Total Funds:		

Monthly Budget Overview

Income

Source	Budget	Actual
Main Income		
Extra Income		
Total Income		

Expences:

Category	Budget	Actual
Total		

Sinking funds

Source	Budget	Actual
Total		

Cash Envelopes:

Category	Budget	Actual
Total		

Total Cost to Withdraw: _____

Debt:

Source	Budget	Actual
Total		

Saving

Category	Add	Balance
Total		

	Budget	Actual
Total Funds:		

Monthly Budget Overview

Income

Source	Budget	Actual
Main Income		
Extra Income		
Total Income		

Expences:

Category	Budget	Actual
Total		

Sinking funds

Source	Budget	Actual
Total		

Cash Envelopes:

Category	Budget	Actual
Total		

Total Cost to Withdraw: _____

Debt:

Source	Budget	Actual
Total		

Saving

Category	Add	Balance
Total		

	Budget	Actual
Total Funds:		

Monthly Budget Overview

Income

Source	Budget	Actual
Main Income		
Extra Income		
Total Income		

Expences:

Category	Budget	Actual
Total		

Sinking funds

Source	Budget	Actual
Total		

Cash Envelopes:

Category	Budget	Actual
Total		

Total Cost to Withdraw: _____

Debt:

Source	Budget	Actual
Total		

Saving

Category	Add	Balance
Total		

	Budget	Actual
Total Funds:		

Monthly Budget Overview

Income

Source	Budget	Actual
Main Income		
Extra Income		
Total Income		

Expences:

Category	Budget	Actual
Total		

Sinking funds

Source	Budget	Actual
Total		

Cash Envelopes:

Category	Budget	Actual
Total		

Debt:

Source	Budget	Actual
Total		

Saving

Category	Add	Balance
Total		

Total Cost to Withdraw: _____

	Budget	Actual
Total Funds:		

Monthly Budget Overview

Income

Source	Budget	Actual
Main Income		
Extra Income		
Total Income		

Expences:

Category	Budget	Actual
Total		

Sinking funds

Source	Budget	Actual
Total		

Cash Envelopes:

Category	Budget	Actual
Total		

Total Cost to Withdraw: _____

Debt:

Source	Budget	Actual
Total		

Saving

Category	Add	Balance
Total		

	Budget	Actual
Total Funds:		

Monthly Budget Overview

Income

Source	Budget	Actual
Main Income		
Extra Income		
Total Income		

Expences:

Category	Budget	Actual
Total		

Sinking funds

Source	Budget	Actual
Total		

Cash Envelopes:

Category	Budget	Actual
Total		

Total Cost to Withdraw: _____

Debt:

Source	Budget	Actual
Total		

Saving

Category	Add	Balance
Total		

	Budget	Actual
Total Funds:		

Monthly Budget Overview

Income

Source	Budget	Actual
Main Income		
Extra Income		
Total Income		

Expences:

Category	Budget	Actual
Total		

Sinking funds

Source	Budget	Actual
Total		

Cash Envelopes:

Category	Budget	Actual
Total		

Total Cost to Withdraw: _____

Debt:

Source	Budget	Actual
Total		

Saving

Category	Add	Balance
Total		

	Budget	Actual
Total Funds:		

Monthly Budget Overview

Income

Source	Budget	Actual
Main Income		
Extra Income		
Total Income		

Expences:

Category	Budget	Actual
Total		

Sinking funds

Source	Budget	Actual
Total		

Cash Envelopes:

Category	Budget	Actual
Total		

Total Cost to Withdraw: _____

Debt:

Source	Budget	Actual
Total		

Saving

Category	Add	Balance
Total		

	Budget	Actual
Total Funds:		

Monthly Budget Overview

Income

Source	Budget	Actual
Main Income		
Extra Income		
Total Income		

Expences:

Category	Budget	Actual
Total		

Sinking funds

Source	Budget	Actual
Total		

Cash Envelopes:

Category	Budget	Actual
Total		

Total Cost to Withdraw: _____

Debt:

Source	Budget	Actual
Total		

Saving

Category	Add	Balance
Total		

	Budget	Actual
Total Funds:		

Monthly Budget Overview

Income

Source	Budget	Actual
Main Income		
Extra Income		
Total Income		

Expences:

Category	Budget	Actual
Total		

Sinking funds

Source	Budget	Actual
Total		

Cash Envelopes:

Category	Budget	Actual
Total		

Total Cost to Withdraw: _____

Debt:

Source	Budget	Actual
Total		

Saving

Category	Add	Balance
Total		

	Budget	Actual
Total Funds:		

Monthly Budget Overview

Income

Source	Budget	Actual
Main Income		
Extra Income		
Total Income		

Expences:

Category	Budget	Actual
Total		

Sinking funds

Source	Budget	Actual
Total		

Cash Envelopes:

Category	Budget	Actual
Total		

Total Cost to Withdraw: _____

Debt:

Source	Budget	Actual
Total		

Saving

Category	Add	Balance
Total		

	Budget	Actual
Total Funds:		

Monthly Budget Overview

Income

Source	Budget	Actual
Main Income		
Extra Income		
Total Income		

Expences:

Category	Budget	Actual
Total		

Sinking funds

Source	Budget	Actual
Total		

Cash Envelopes:

Category	Budget	Actual
Total		

Total Cost to Withdraw: _____

Debt:

Source	Budget	Actual
Total		

Saving

Category	Add	Balance
Total		

	Budget	Actual
Total Funds:		

Monthly Budget Overview

Income

Source	Budget	Actual
Main Income		
Extra Income		
Total Income		

Expences:

Category	Budget	Actual
Total		

Sinking funds

Source	Budget	Actual
Total		

Cash Envelopes:

Category	Budget	Actual
Total		

Total Cost to Withdraw: _____

Debt:

Source	Budget	Actual
Total		

Saving

Category	Add	Balance
Total		

	Budget	Actual
Total Funds:		

Monthly Budget Overview

Income

Source	Budget	Actual
Main Income		
Extra Income		
Total Income		

Expences:

Category	Budget	Actual
Total		

Sinking funds

Source	Budget	Actual
Total		

Cash Envelopes:

Category	Budget	Actual
Total		

Total Cost to Withdraw: _____

Debt:

Source	Budget	Actual
Total		

Saving

Category	Add	Balance
Total		

	Budget	Actual
Total Funds:		

Monthly Budget Overview

Income

Source	Budget	Actual
Main Income		
Extra Income		
Total Income		

Expences:

Category	Budget	Actual
Total		

Sinking funds

Source	Budget	Actual
Total		

Cash Envelopes:

Category	Budget	Actual
Total		

Total Cost to Withdraw: _____

Debt:

Source	Budget	Actual
Total		

Saving

Category	Add	Balance
Total		

	Budget	Actual
Total Funds:		

Monthly Budget Overview

Income

Source	Budget	Actual
Main Income		
Extra Income		
Total Income		

Expences:

Category	Budget	Actual
Total		

Sinking funds

Source	Budget	Actual
Total		

Cash Envelopes:

Category	Budget	Actual
Total		

Total Cost to Withdraw: _____

Debt:

Source	Budget	Actual
Total		

Saving

Category	Add	Balance
Total		

	Budget	Actual
Total Funds:		

Monthly Budget Overview

Income

Source	Budget	Actual
Main Income		
Extra Income		
Total Income		

Expences:

Category	Budget	Actual
Total		

Sinking funds

Source	Budget	Actual
Total		

Cash Envelopes:

Category	Budget	Actual
Total		

Total Cost to Withdraw: _____

Debt:

Source	Budget	Actual
Total		

Saving

Category	Add	Balance
Total		

	Budget	Actual
Total Funds:		

Monthly Budget Overview

Income

Source	Budget	Actual
Main Income		
Extra Income		
Total Income		

Expences:

Category	Budget	Actual
Total		

Sinking funds

Source	Budget	Actual
Total		

Cash Envelopes:

Category	Budget	Actual
Total		

Debt:

Source	Budget	Actual
Total		

Saving

Category	Add	Balance
Total		

Total Cost to Withdraw: _____

	Budget	Actual
Total Funds:		

Monthly Budget Overview

Income

Source	Budget	Actual
Main Income		
Extra Income		
Total Income		

Expences:

Category	Budget	Actual
Total		

Sinking funds

Source	Budget	Actual
Total		

Cash Envelopes:

Category	Budget	Actual
Total		

Total Cost to Withdraw: _____

Debt:

Source	Budget	Actual
Total		

Saving

Category	Add	Balance
Total		

	Budget	Actual
Total Funds:		

Monthly Budget Overview

Income

Source	Budget	Actual
Main Income		
Extra Income		
Total Income		

Expences:

Category	Budget	Actual
Total		

Sinking funds

Source	Budget	Actual
Total		

Cash Envelopes:

Category	Budget	Actual
Total		

Total Cost to Withdraw: _____

Debt:

Source	Budget	Actual
Total		

Saving

Category	Add	Balance
Total		

	Budget	Actual
Total Funds:		

Monthly Budget Overview

Income

Source	Budget	Actual
Main Income		
Extra Income		
Total Income		

Expences:

Category	Budget	Actual
Total		

Sinking funds

Source	Budget	Actual
Total		

Cash Envelopes:

Category	Budget	Actual
Total		

Total Cost to Withdraw: _____

Debt:

Source	Budget	Actual
Total		

Saving

Category	Add	Balance
Total		

	Budget	Actual
Total Funds:		

Monthly Budget Overview

Income

Source	Budget	Actual
Main Income		
Extra Income		
Total Income		

Expences:

Category	Budget	Actual
Total		

Sinking funds

Source	Budget	Actual
Total		

Cash Envelopes:

Category	Budget	Actual
Total		

Total Cost to Withdraw: _____

Debt:

Source	Budget	Actual
Total		

Saving

Category	Add	Balance
Total		

	Budget	Actual
Total Funds:		

Monthly Budget Overview

Income

Source	Budget	Actual
Main Income		
Extra Income		
Total Income		

Expences:

Category	Budget	Actual
Total		

Sinking funds

Source	Budget	Actual
Total		

Cash Envelopes:

Category	Budget	Actual
Total		

Total Cost to Withdraw: _____

Debt:

Source	Budget	Actual
Total		

Saving

Category	Add	Balance
Total		

	Budget	Actual
Total Funds:		

Monthly Budget Overview

Income

Source	Budget	Actual
Main Income		
Extra Income		
Total Income		

Expences:

Category	Budget	Actual
Total		

Sinking funds

Source	Budget	Actual
Total		

Cash Envelopes:

Category	Budget	Actual
Total		

Total Cost to Withdraw: _____

Debt:

Source	Budget	Actual
Total		

Saving

Category	Add	Balance
Total		

	Budget	Actual
Total Funds:		

Monthly Budget Overview

Income

Source	Budget	Actual
Main Income		
Extra Income		
Total Income		

Expences:

Category	Budget	Actual
Total		

Sinking funds

Source	Budget	Actual
Total		

Cash Envelopes:

Category	Budget	Actual
Total		

Total Cost to Withdraw: _____

Debt:

Source	Budget	Actual
Total		

Saving

Category	Add	Balance
Total		

	Budget	Actual
Total Funds:		

Monthly Budget Overview

Income

Source	Budget	Actual
Main Income		
Extra Income		
Total Income		

Expences:

Category	Budget	Actual
Total		

Sinking funds

Source	Budget	Actual
Total		

Cash Envelopes:

Category	Budget	Actual
Total		

Total Cost to Withdraw: _____

Debt:

Source	Budget	Actual
Total		

Saving

Category	Add	Balance
Total		

	Budget	Actual
Total Funds:		

Monthly Budget Overview

Income

Source	Budget	Actual
Main Income		
Extra Income		
Total Income		

Expences:

Category	Budget	Actual
Total		

Sinking funds

Source	Budget	Actual
Total		

Cash Envelopes:

Category	Budget	Actual
Total		

Total Cost to Withdraw: _____

Debt:

Source	Budget	Actual
Total		

Saving

Category	Add	Balance
Total		

	Budget	Actual
Total Funds:		

Monthly Budget Overview

Income

Source	Budget	Actual
Main Income		
Extra Income		
Total Income		

Expences:

Category	Budget	Actual
Total		

Sinking funds

Source	Budget	Actual
Total		

Cash Envelopes:

Category	Budget	Actual
Total		

Total Cost to Withdraw: _____

Debt:

Source	Budget	Actual
Total		

Saving

Category	Add	Balance
Total		

	Budget	Actual
Total Funds:		

Monthly Budget Overview

Income

Source	Budget	Actual
Main Income		
Extra Income		
Total Income		

Expences:

Category	Budget	Actual
Total		

Sinking funds

Source	Budget	Actual
Total		

Cash Envelopes:

Category	Budget	Actual
Total		

Total Cost to Withdraw: _____

Debt:

Source	Budget	Actual
Total		

Saving

Category	Add	Balance
Total		

	Budget	Actual
Total Funds:		

Monthly Budget Overview

Income

Source	Budget	Actual
Main Income		
Extra Income		
Total Income		

Expences:

Category	Budget	Actual
Total		

Sinking funds

Source	Budget	Actual
Total		

Cash Envelopes:

Category	Budget	Actual
Total		

Total Cost to Withdraw: _____

Debt:

Source	Budget	Actual
Total		

Saving

Category	Add	Balance
Total		

	Budget	Actual
Total Funds:		

Monthly Budget Overview

Income

Source	Budget	Actual
Main Income		
Extra Income		
Total Income		

Expences:

Category	Budget	Actual
Total		

Sinking funds

Source	Budget	Actual
Total		

Cash Envelopes:

Category	Budget	Actual
Total		

Total Cost to Withdraw: _____

Debt:

Source	Budget	Actual
Total		

Saving

Category	Add	Balance
Total		

	Budget	Actual
Total Funds:		

Monthly Budget Overview

Income

Source	Budget	Actual
Main Income		
Extra Income		
Total Income		

Expences:

Category	Budget	Actual
Total		

Sinking funds

Source	Budget	Actual
Total		

Cash Envelopes:

Category	Budget	Actual
Total		

Total Cost to Withdraw: _____

Debt:

Source	Budget	Actual
Total		

Saving

Category	Add	Balance
Total		

	Budget	Actual
Total Funds:		

Monthly Budget Overview

Income

Source	Budget	Actual
Main Income		
Extra Income		
Total Income		

Expences:

Category	Budget	Actual
Total		

Sinking funds

Source	Budget	Actual
Total		

Cash Envelopes:

Category	Budget	Actual
Total		

Total Cost to Withdraw: _____

Debt:

Source	Budget	Actual
Total		

Saving

Category	Add	Balance
Total		

	Budget	Actual
Total Funds:		

Monthly Budget Overview

Income

Source	Budget	Actual
Main Income		
Extra Income		
Total Income		

Expences:

Category	Budget	Actual
Total		

Sinking funds

Source	Budget	Actual
Total		

Cash Envelopes:

Category	Budget	Actual
Total		

Total Cost to Withdraw: _____

Debt:

Source	Budget	Actual
Total		

Saving

Category	Add	Balance
Total		

	Budget	Actual
Total Funds:		

Monthly Budget Overview

Income

Source	Budget	Actual
Main Income		
Extra Income		
Total Income		

Expences:

Category	Budget	Actual
Total		

Sinking funds

Source	Budget	Actual
Total		

Cash Envelopes:

Category	Budget	Actual
Total		

Total Cost to Withdraw: _____

Debt:

Source	Budget	Actual
Total		

Saving

Category	Add	Balance
Total		

	Budget	Actual
Total Funds:		

Monthly Budget Overview

Income

Source	Budget	Actual
Main Income		
Extra Income		
Total Income		

Expences:

Category	Budget	Actual
Total		

Sinking funds

Source	Budget	Actual
Total		

Cash Envelopes:

Category	Budget	Actual
Total		

Total Cost to Withdraw: _____

Debt:

Source	Budget	Actual
Total		

Saving

Category	Add	Balance
Total		

	Budget	Actual
Total Funds:		

Monthly Budget Overview

Income

Source	Budget	Actual
Main Income		
Extra Income		
Total Income		

Expences:

Category	Budget	Actual
Total		

Sinking funds

Source	Budget	Actual
Total		

Cash Envelopes:

Category	Budget	Actual
Total		

Total Cost to Withdraw: _____

Debt:

Source	Budget	Actual
Total		

Saving

Category	Add	Balance
Total		

	Budget	Actual
Total Funds:		

Monthly Budget Overview

Income

Source	Budget	Actual
Main Income		
Extra Income		
Total Income		

Expences:

Category	Budget	Actual
Total		

Sinking funds

Source	Budget	Actual
Total		

Cash Envelopes:

Category	Budget	Actual
Total		

Total Cost to Withdraw: _____

Debt:

Source	Budget	Actual
Total		

Saving

Category	Add	Balance
Total		

	Budget	Actual
Total Funds:		

Monthly Budget Overview

Income

Source	Budget	Actual
Main Income		
Extra Income		
Total Income		

Expences:

Category	Budget	Actual
Total		

Sinking funds

Source	Budget	Actual
Total		

Cash Envelopes:

Category	Budget	Actual
Total		

Total Cost to Withdraw: _____

Debt:

Source	Budget	Actual
Total		

Saving

Category	Add	Balance
Total		

	Budget	Actual
Total Funds:		

Monthly Budget Overview

Income

Source	Budget	Actual
Main Income		
Extra Income		
Total Income		

Expences:

Category	Budget	Actual
Total		

Sinking funds

Source	Budget	Actual
Total		

Cash Envelopes:

Category	Budget	Actual
Total		

Total Cost to Withdraw: _____

Debt:

Source	Budget	Actual
Total		

Saving

Category	Add	Balance
Total		

	Budget	Actual
Total Funds:		

Monthly Budget Overview

Income

Source	Budget	Actual
Main Income		
Extra Income		
Total Income		

Expences:

Category	Budget	Actual
Total		

Sinking funds

Source	Budget	Actual
Total		

Cash Envelopes:

Category	Budget	Actual
Total		

Total Cost to Withdraw: _____

Debt:

Source	Budget	Actual
Total		

Saving

Category	Add	Balance
Total		

	Budget	Actual
Total Funds:		

Monthly Budget Overview

Income

Source	Budget	Actual
Main Income		
Extra Income		
Total Income		

Expences:

Category	Budget	Actual
Total		

Sinking funds

Source	Budget	Actual
Total		

Cash Envelopes:

Category	Budget	Actual
Total		

Debt:

Source	Budget	Actual
Total		

Saving

Category	Add	Balance
Total		

Total Cost to Withdraw: _____

	Budget	Actual
Total Funds:		

Monthly Budget Overview

Income

Source	Budget	Actual
Main Income		
Extra Income		
Total Income		

Expences:

Category	Budget	Actual
Total		

Sinking funds

Source	Budget	Actual
Total		

Cash Envelopes:

Category	Budget	Actual
Total		

Total Cost to Withdraw: _____

Debt:

Source	Budget	Actual
Total		

Saving

Category	Add	Balance
Total		

	Budget	Actual
Total Funds:		

Monthly Budget Overview

Income

Source	Budget	Actual
Main Income		
Extra Income		
Total Income		

Expences:

Category	Budget	Actual
Total		

Sinking funds

Source	Budget	Actual
Total		

Cash Envelopes:

Category	Budget	Actual
Total		

Debt:

Source	Budget	Actual
Total		

Saving

Category	Add	Balance
Total		

Total Cost to Withdraw: _____

	Budget	Actual
Total Funds:		

Monthly Budget Overview

Income

Source	Budget	Actual
Main Income		
Extra Income		
Total Income		

Expences:

Category	Budget	Actual
Total		

Sinking funds

Source	Budget	Actual
Total		

Cash Envelopes:

Category	Budget	Actual
Total		

Total Cost to Withdraw: _____

Debt:

Source	Budget	Actual
Total		

Saving

Category	Add	Balance
Total		

	Budget	Actual
Total Funds:		

Monthly Budget Overview

Income

Source	Budget	Actual
Main Income		
Extra Income		
Total Income		

Expences:

Category	Budget	Actual
Total		

Sinking funds

Source	Budget	Actual
Total		

Cash Envelopes:

Category	Budget	Actual
Total		

Total Cost to Withdraw: _____

Debt:

Source	Budget	Actual
Total		

Saving

Category	Add	Balance
Total		

	Budget	Actual
Total Funds:		

Monthly Budget Overview

Income

Source	Budget	Actual
Main Income		
Extra Income		
Total Income		

Expences:

Category	Budget	Actual
Total		

Sinking funds

Source	Budget	Actual
Total		

Cash Envelopes:

Category	Budget	Actual
Total		

Total Cost to Withdraw: _____

Debt:

Source	Budget	Actual
Total		

Saving

Category	Add	Balance
Total		

	Budget	Actual
Total Funds:		

Monthly Budget Overview

Income

Source	Budget	Actual
Main Income		
Extra Income		
Total Income		

Expences:

Category	Budget	Actual
Total		

Sinking funds

Source	Budget	Actual
Total		

Cash Envelopes:

Category	Budget	Actual
Total		

Total Cost to Withdraw: _____

Debt:

Source	Budget	Actual
Total		

Saving

Category	Add	Balance
Total		

	Budget	Actual
Total Funds:		

Monthly Budget Overview

Income

Source	Budget	Actual
Main Income		
Extra Income		
Total Income		

Expences:

Category	Budget	Actual
Total		

Sinking funds

Source	Budget	Actual
Total		

Cash Envelopes:

Category	Budget	Actual
Total		

Total Cost to Withdraw: _____

Debt:

Source	Budget	Actual
Total		

Saving

Category	Add	Balance
Total		

	Budget	Actual
Total Funds:		

Monthly Budget Overview

Income

Source	Budget	Actual
Main Income		
Extra Income		
Total Income		

Expences:

Category	Budget	Actual
Total		

Sinking funds

Source	Budget	Actual
Total		

Cash Envelopes:

Category	Budget	Actual
Total		

Total Cost to Withdraw: _____

Debt:

Source	Budget	Actual
Total		

Saving

Category	Add	Balance
Total		

	Budget	Actual
Total Funds:		

Monthly Budget Overview

Income

Source	Budget	Actual
Main Income		
Extra Income		
Total Income		

Expences:

Category	Budget	Actual
Total		

Sinking funds

Source	Budget	Actual
Total		

Cash Envelopes:

Category	Budget	Actual
Total		

Debt:

Source	Budget	Actual
Total		

Saving

Category	Add	Balance
Total		

Total Cost to Withdraw: _____

	Budget	Actual
Total Funds:		

Monthly Budget Overview

Income

Source	Budget	Actual
Main Income		
Extra Income		
Total Income		

Expences:

Category	Budget	Actual
Total		

Sinking funds

Source	Budget	Actual
Total		

Cash Envelopes:

Category	Budget	Actual
Total		

Total Cost to Withdraw: _____

Debt:

Source	Budget	Actual
Total		

Saving

Category	Add	Balance
Total		

	Budget	Actual
Total Funds:		

Monthly Budget Overview

Income

Source	Budget	Actual
Main Income		
Extra Income		
Total Income		

Expences:

Category	Budget	Actual
Total		

Sinking funds

Source	Budget	Actual
Total		

Cash Envelopes:

Category	Budget	Actual
Total		

Total Cost to Withdraw: _____

Debt:

Source	Budget	Actual
Total		

Saving

Category	Add	Balance
Total		

	Budget	Actual
Total Funds:		

Monthly Budget Overview

Income

Source	Budget	Actual
Main Income		
Extra Income		
Total Income		

Expences:

Category	Budget	Actual
Total		

Sinking funds

Source	Budget	Actual
Total		

Cash Envelopes:

Category	Budget	Actual
Total		

Total Cost to Withdraw: _____

Debt:

Source	Budget	Actual
Total		

Saving

Category	Add	Balance
Total		

	Budget	Actual
Total Funds:		

Monthly Budget Overview

Income

Source	Budget	Actual
Main Income		
Extra Income		
Total Income		

Expences:

Category	Budget	Actual
Total		

Sinking funds

Source	Budget	Actual
Total		

Cash Envelopes:

Category	Budget	Actual
Total		

Total Cost to Withdraw: _____

Debt:

Source	Budget	Actual
Total		

Saving

Category	Add	Balance
Total		

	Budget	Actual
Total Funds:		

Monthly Budget Overview

Income

Source	Budget	Actual
Main Income		
Extra Income		
Total Income		

Expences:

Category	Budget	Actual
Total		

Sinking funds

Source	Budget	Actual
Total		

Cash Envelopes:

Category	Budget	Actual
Total		

Total Cost to Withdraw: _____

Debt:

Source	Budget	Actual
Total		

Saving

Category	Add	Balance
Total		

	Budget	Actual
Total Funds:		

Monthly Budget Overview

Income

Source	Budget	Actual
Main Income		
Extra Income		
Total Income		

Expences:

Category	Budget	Actual
Total		

Sinking funds

Source	Budget	Actual
Total		

Cash Envelopes:

Category	Budget	Actual
Total		

Total Cost to Withdraw: _____

Debt:

Source	Budget	Actual
Total		

Saving

Category	Add	Balance
Total		

	Budget	Actual
Total Funds:		

Monthly Budget Overview

Income

Source	Budget	Actual
Main Income		
Extra Income		
Total Income		

Expences:

Category	Budget	Actual
Total		

Sinking funds

Source	Budget	Actual
Total		

Cash Envelopes:

Category	Budget	Actual
Total		

Debt:

Source	Budget	Actual
Total		

Saving

Category	Add	Balance
Total		

Total Cost to Withdraw: _____

	Budget	Actual
Total Funds:		

Monthly Budget Overview

Income

Source	Budget	Actual
Main Income		
Extra Income		
Total Income		

Expences:

Category	Budget	Actual
Total		

Sinking funds

Source	Budget	Actual
Total		

Cash Envelopes:

Category	Budget	Actual
Total		

Total Cost to Withdraw: _____

Debt:

Source	Budget	Actual
Total		

Saving

Category	Add	Balance
Total		

	Budget	Actual
Total Funds:		

Monthly Budget Overview

Income

Source	Budget	Actual
Main Income		
Extra Income		
Total Income		

Expences:

Category	Budget	Actual
Total		

Sinking funds

Source	Budget	Actual
Total		

Cash Envelopes:

Category	Budget	Actual
Total		

Total Cost to Withdraw: _____

Debt:

Source	Budget	Actual
Total		

Saving

Category	Add	Balance
Total		

	Budget	Actual
Total Funds:		

Monthly Budget Overview

Income

Source	Budget	Actual
Main Income		
Extra Income		
Total Income		

Expences:

Category	Budget	Actual
Total		

Sinking funds

Source	Budget	Actual
Total		

Cash Envelopes:

Category	Budget	Actual
Total		

Total Cost to Withdraw: _____

Debt:

Source	Budget	Actual
Total		

Saving

Category	Add	Balance
Total		

	Budget	Actual
Total Funds:		

Monthly Budget Overview

Income

Source	Budget	Actual
Main Income		
Extra Income		
Total Income		

Expences:

Category	Budget	Actual
Total		

Sinking funds

Source	Budget	Actual
Total		

Cash Envelopes:

Category	Budget	Actual
Total		

Debt:

Source	Budget	Actual
Total		

Saving

Category	Add	Balance
Total		

Total Cost to Withdraw: _____

	Budget	Actual
Total Funds:		

Monthly Budget Overview

Income

Source	Budget	Actual
Main Income		
Extra Income		
Total Income		

Expences:

Category	Budget	Actual
Total		

Sinking funds

Source	Budget	Actual
Total		

Cash Envelopes:

Category	Budget	Actual
Total		

Debt:

Source	Budget	Actual
Total		

Saving

Category	Add	Balance
Total		

Total Cost to Withdraw: _____

	Budget	Actual
Total Funds:		

Monthly Budget Overview

Income

Source	Budget	Actual
Main Income		
Extra Income		
Total Income		

Expences:

Category	Budget	Actual
Total		

Sinking funds

Source	Budget	Actual
Total		

Cash Envelopes:

Category	Budget	Actual
Total		

Total Cost to Withdraw: _____

Debt:

Source	Budget	Actual
Total		

Saving

Category	Add	Balance
Total		

	Budget	Actual
Total Funds:		

Monthly Budget Overview

Income

Source	Budget	Actual
Main Income		
Extra Income		
Total Income		

Expences:

Category	Budget	Actual
Total		

Sinking funds

Source	Budget	Actual
Total		

Cash Envelopes:

Category	Budget	Actual
Total		

Total Cost to Withdraw: _____

Debt:

Source	Budget	Actual
Total		

Saving

Category	Add	Balance
Total		

	Budget	Actual
Total Funds:		

Monthly Budget Overview

Income

Source	Budget	Actual
Main Income		
Extra Income		
Total Income		

Expences:

Category	Budget	Actual
Total		

Sinking funds

Source	Budget	Actual
Total		

Cash Envelopes:

Category	Budget	Actual
Total		

Total Cost to Withdraw: _____

Debt:

Source	Budget	Actual
Total		

Saving

Category	Add	Balance
Total		

	Budget	Actual
Total Funds:		

Monthly Budget Overview

Income

Source	Budget	Actual
Main Income		
Extra Income		
Total Income		

Expences:

Category	Budget	Actual
Total		

Sinking funds

Source	Budget	Actual
Total		

Cash Envelopes:

Category	Budget	Actual
Total		

Total Cost to Withdraw: _____

Debt:

Source	Budget	Actual
Total		

Saving

Category	Add	Balance
Total		

	Budget	Actual
Total Funds:		

Monthly Budget Overview

Income

Source	Budget	Actual
Main Income		
Extra Income		
Total Income		

Expences:

Category	Budget	Actual
Total		

Sinking funds

Source	Budget	Actual
Total		

Cash Envelopes:

Category	Budget	Actual
Total		

Total Cost to Withdraw: _____

Debt:

Source	Budget	Actual
Total		

Saving

Category	Add	Balance
Total		

	Budget	Actual
Total Funds:		

Monthly Budget Overview

Income

Source	Budget	Actual
Main Income		
Extra Income		
Total Income		

Expences:

Category	Budget	Actual
Total		

Sinking funds

Source	Budget	Actual
Total		

Cash Envelopes:

Category	Budget	Actual
Total		

Total Cost to Withdraw: _____

Debt:

Source	Budget	Actual
Total		

Saving

Category	Add	Balance
Total		

	Budget	Actual
Total Funds:		

Monthly Budget Overview

Income

Source	Budget	Actual
Main Income		
Extra Income		
Total Income		

Expences:

Category	Budget	Actual
Total		

Sinking funds

Source	Budget	Actual
Total		

Cash Envelopes:

Category	Budget	Actual
Total		

Debt:

Source	Budget	Actual
Total		

Saving

Category	Add	Balance
Total		

Total Cost to Withdraw: _____

	Budget	Actual
Total Funds:		

Monthly Budget Overview

Income

Source	Budget	Actual
Main Income		
Extra Income		
Total Income		

Expences:

Category	Budget	Actual
Total		

Sinking funds

Source	Budget	Actual
Total		

Cash Envelopes:

Category	Budget	Actual
Total		

Total Cost to Withdraw: _____

Debt:

Source	Budget	Actual
Total		

Saving

Category	Add	Balance
Total		

	Budget	Actual
Total Funds:		

Monthly Budget Overview

Income

Source	Budget	Actual
Main Income		
Extra Income		
Total Income		

Expences:

Category	Budget	Actual
Total		

Sinking funds

Source	Budget	Actual
Total		

Cash Envelopes:

Category	Budget	Actual
Total		

Total Cost to Withdraw: _____

Debt:

Source	Budget	Actual
Total		

Saving

Category	Add	Balance
Total		

	Budget	Actual
Total Funds:		

Monthly Budget Overview

Income

Source	Budget	Actual
Main Income		
Extra Income		
Total Income		

Expences:

Category	Budget	Actual
Total		

Sinking funds

Source	Budget	Actual
Total		

Cash Envelopes:

Category	Budget	Actual
Total		

Total Cost to Withdraw: _____

Debt:

Source	Budget	Actual
Total		

Saving

Category	Add	Balance
Total		

	Budget	Actual
Total Funds:		

Monthly Budget Overview

Income

Source	Budget	Actual
Main Income		
Extra Income		
Total Income		

Expences:

Category	Budget	Actual
Total		

Sinking funds

Source	Budget	Actual
Total		

Cash Envelopes:

Category	Budget	Actual
Total		

Total Cost to Withdraw: _____

Debt:

Source	Budget	Actual
Total		

Saving

Category	Add	Balance
Total		

	Budget	Actual
Total Funds:		

Monthly Budget Overview

Income

Source	Budget	Actual
Main Income		
Extra Income		
Total Income		

Expences:

Category	Budget	Actual
Total		

Sinking funds

Source	Budget	Actual
Total		

Cash Envelopes:

Category	Budget	Actual
Total		

Total Cost to Withdraw: _____

Debt:

Source	Budget	Actual
Total		

Saving

Category	Add	Balance
Total		

	Budget	Actual
Total Funds:		

Monthly Budget Overview

Income

Source	Budget	Actual
Main Income		
Extra Income		
Total Income		

Expences:

Category	Budget	Actual
Total		

Sinking funds

Source	Budget	Actual
Total		

Cash Envelopes:

Category	Budget	Actual
Total		

Total Cost to Withdraw: _____

Debt:

Source	Budget	Actual
Total		

Saving

Category	Add	Balance
Total		

	Budget	Actual
Total Funds:		

Monthly Budget Overview

Income

Source	Budget	Actual
Main Income		
Extra Income		
Total Income		

Expences:

Category	Budget	Actual
Total		

Sinking funds

Source	Budget	Actual
Total		

Cash Envelopes:

Category	Budget	Actual
Total		

Total Cost to Withdraw: _____

Debt:

Source	Budget	Actual
Total		

Saving

Category	Add	Balance
Total		

	Budget	Actual
Total Funds:		

Monthly Budget Overview

Income

Source	Budget	Actual
Main Income		
Extra Income		
Total Income		

Expences:

Category	Budget	Actual
Total		

Sinking funds

Source	Budget	Actual
Total		

Cash Envelopes:

Category	Budget	Actual
Total		

Total Cost to Withdraw: _____

Debt:

Source	Budget	Actual
Total		

Saving

Category	Add	Balance
Total		

	Budget	Actual
Total Funds:		

Monthly Budget Overview

Income

Source	Budget	Actual
Main Income		
Extra Income		
Total Income		

Expences:

Category	Budget	Actual
Total		

Sinking funds

Source	Budget	Actual
Total		

Cash Envelopes:

Category	Budget	Actual
Total		

Total Cost to Withdraw: _____

Debt:

Source	Budget	Actual
Total		

Saving

Category	Add	Balance
Total		

	Budget	Actual
Total Funds:		

Monthly Budget Overview

Income

Source	Budget	Actual
Main Income		
Extra Income		
Total Income		

Expences:

Category	Budget	Actual
Total		

Sinking funds

Source	Budget	Actual
Total		

Cash Envelopes:

Category	Budget	Actual
Total		

Total Cost to Withdraw: _____

Debt:

Source	Budget	Actual
Total		

Saving

Category	Add	Balance
Total		

	Budget	Actual
Total Funds:		

Monthly Budget Overview

Income

Source	Budget	Actual
Main Income		
Extra Income		
Total Income		

Expences:

Category	Budget	Actual
Total		

Sinking funds

Source	Budget	Actual
Total		

Cash Envelopes:

Category	Budget	Actual
Total		

Total Cost to Withdraw: _____

Debt:

Source	Budget	Actual
Total		

Saving

Category	Add	Balance
Total		

	Budget	Actual
Total Funds:		

Monthly Budget Overview

Income

Source	Budget	Actual
Main Income		
Extra Income		
Total Income		

Expences:

Category	Budget	Actual
Total		

Sinking funds

Source	Budget	Actual
Total		

Cash Envelopes:

Category	Budget	Actual
Total		

Total Cost to Withdraw: _____

Debt:

Source	Budget	Actual
Total		

Saving

Category	Add	Balance
Total		

	Budget	Actual
Total Funds:		

Monthly Budget Overview

Income

Source	Budget	Actual
Main Income		
Extra Income		
Total Income		

Expences:

Category	Budget	Actual
Total		

Sinking funds

Source	Budget	Actual
Total		

Cash Envelopes:

Category	Budget	Actual
Total		

Total Cost to Withdraw: _____

Debt:

Source	Budget	Actual
Total		

Saving

Category	Add	Balance
Total		

	Budget	Actual
Total Funds:		

Monthly Budget Overview

Income

Source	Budget	Actual
Main Income		
Extra Income		
Total Income		

Expences:

Category	Budget	Actual
Total		

Sinking funds

Source	Budget	Actual
Total		

Cash Envelopes:

Category	Budget	Actual
Total		

Total Cost to Withdraw: _____

Debt:

Source	Budget	Actual
Total		

Saving

Category	Add	Balance
Total		

	Budget	Actual
Total Funds:		

Monthly Budget Overview

Income

Source	Budget	Actual
Main Income		
Extra Income		
Total Income		

Expences:

Category	Budget	Actual
Total		

Sinking funds

Source	Budget	Actual
Total		

Cash Envelopes:

Category	Budget	Actual
Total		

Total Cost to Withdraw: _____

Debt:

Source	Budget	Actual
Total		

Saving

Category	Add	Balance
Total		

	Budget	Actual
Total Funds:		

Monthly Budget Overview

Income

Source	Budget	Actual
Main Income		
Extra Income		
Total Income		

Expences:

Category	Budget	Actual
Total		

Sinking funds

Source	Budget	Actual
Total		

Cash Envelopes:

Category	Budget	Actual
Total		

Total Cost to Withdraw: _____

Debt:

Source	Budget	Actual
Total		

Saving

Category	Add	Balance
Total		

	Budget	Actual
Total Funds:		

Monthly Budget Overview

Income

Source	Budget	Actual
Main Income		
Extra Income		
Total Income		

Expences:

Category	Budget	Actual
Total		

Sinking funds

Source	Budget	Actual
Total		

Cash Envelopes:

Category	Budget	Actual
Total		

Total Cost to Withdraw: _____

Debt:

Source	Budget	Actual
Total		

Saving

Category	Add	Balance
Total		

	Budget	Actual
Total Funds:		

Monthly Budget Overview

Income

Source	Budget	Actual
Main Income		
Extra Income		
Total Income		

Expences:

Category	Budget	Actual
Total		

Sinking funds

Source	Budget	Actual
Total		

Cash Envelopes:

Category	Budget	Actual
Total		

Total Cost to Withdraw: _____

Debt:

Source	Budget	Actual
Total		

Saving

Category	Add	Balance
Total		

	Budget	Actual
Total Funds:		

Monthly Budget Overview

Income

Source	Budget	Actual
Main Income		
Extra Income		
Total Income		

Expences:

Category	Budget	Actual
Total		

Sinking funds

Source	Budget	Actual
Total		

Cash Envelopes:

Category	Budget	Actual
Total		

Total Cost to Withdraw: _____

Debt:

Source	Budget	Actual
Total		

Saving

Category	Add	Balance
Total		

	Budget	Actual
Total Funds:		

Monthly Budget Overview

Income

Source	Budget	Actual
Main Income		
Extra Income		
Total Income		

Expences:

Category	Budget	Actual
Total		

Sinking funds

Source	Budget	Actual
Total		

Cash Envelopes:

Category	Budget	Actual
Total		

Total Cost to Withdraw: _____

Debt:

Source	Budget	Actual
Total		

Saving

Category	Add	Balance
Total		

	Budget	Actual
Total Funds:		

Monthly Budget Overview

Income

Source	Budget	Actual
Main Income		
Extra Income		
Total Income		

Expences:

Category	Budget	Actual
Total		

Sinking funds

Source	Budget	Actual
Total		

Cash Envelopes:

Category	Budget	Actual
Total		

Total Cost to Withdraw: _____

Debt:

Source	Budget	Actual
Total		

Saving

Category	Add	Balance
Total		

	Budget	Actual
Total Funds:		

Monthly Budget Overview

Income

Source	Budget	Actual
Main Income		
Extra Income		
Total Income		

Expences:

Category	Budget	Actual
Total		

Sinking funds

Source	Budget	Actual
Total		

Cash Envelopes:

Category	Budget	Actual
Total		

Debt:

Source	Budget	Actual
Total		

Saving

Category	Add	Balance
Total		

Total Cost to Withdraw: _____

	Budget	Actual
Total Funds:		

Monthly Budget Overview

Income

Source	Budget	Actual
Main Income		
Extra Income		
Total Income		

Expences:

Category	Budget	Actual
Total		

Sinking funds

Source	Budget	Actual
Total		

Cash Envelopes:

Category	Budget	Actual
Total		

Total Cost to Withdraw: _____

Debt:

Source	Budget	Actual
Total		

Saving

Category	Add	Balance
Total		

	Budget	Actual
Total Funds:		

Monthly Budget Overview

Income

Source	Budget	Actual
Main Income		
Extra Income		
Total Income		

Expences:

Category	Budget	Actual
Total		

Sinking funds

Source	Budget	Actual
Total		

Cash Envelopes:

Category	Budget	Actual
Total		

Total Cost to Withdraw: _____

Debt:

Source	Budget	Actual
Total		

Saving

Category	Add	Balance
Total		

	Budget	Actual
Total Funds:		

Monthly Budget Overview

Income

Source	Budget	Actual
Main Income		
Extra Income		
Total Income		

Expences:

Category	Budget	Actual
Total		

Sinking funds

Source	Budget	Actual
Total		

Cash Envelopes:

Category	Budget	Actual
Total		

Total Cost to Withdraw: _____

Debt:

Source	Budget	Actual
Total		

Saving

Category	Add	Balance
Total		

	Budget	Actual
Total Funds:		

Monthly Budget Overview

Income

Source	Budget	Actual
Main Income		
Extra Income		
Total Income		

Expences:

Category	Budget	Actual
Total		

Sinking funds

Source	Budget	Actual
Total		

Cash Envelopes:

Category	Budget	Actual
Total		

Total Cost to Withdraw: _____

Debt:

Source	Budget	Actual
Total		

Saving

Category	Add	Balance
Total		

	Budget	Actual
Total Funds:		

Monthly Budget Overview

Income

Source	Budget	Actual
Main Income		
Extra Income		
Total Income		

Expences:

Category	Budget	Actual
Total		

Sinking funds

Source	Budget	Actual
Total		

Cash Envelopes:

Category	Budget	Actual
Total		

Total Cost to Withdraw: _____

Debt:

Source	Budget	Actual
Total		

Saving

Category	Add	Balance
Total		

	Budget	Actual
Total Funds:		

Monthly Budget Overview

Income

Source	Budget	Actual
Main Income		
Extra Income		
Total Income		

Expences:

Category	Budget	Actual
Total		

Sinking funds

Source	Budget	Actual
Total		

Cash Envelopes:

Category	Budget	Actual
Total		

Total Cost to Withdraw: _____

Debt:

Source	Budget	Actual
Total		

Saving

Category	Add	Balance
Total		

	Budget	Actual
Total Funds:		

Monthly Budget Overview

Income

Source	Budget	Actual
Main Income		
Extra Income		
Total Income		

Expences:

Category	Budget	Actual
Total		

Sinking funds

Source	Budget	Actual
Total		

Cash Envelopes:

Category	Budget	Actual
Total		

Total Cost to Withdraw: _____

Debt:

Source	Budget	Actual
Total		

Saving

Category	Add	Balance
Total		

	Budget	Actual
Total Funds:		

Monthly Budget Overview

Income

Source	Budget	Actual
Main Income		
Extra Income		
Total Income		

Expences:

Category	Budget	Actual
Total		

Sinking funds

Source	Budget	Actual
Total		

Cash Envelopes:

Category	Budget	Actual
Total		

Total Cost to Withdraw: _____

Debt:

Source	Budget	Actual
Total		

Saving

Category	Add	Balance
Total		

	Budget	Actual
Total Funds:		

Monthly Budget Overview

Income

Source	Budget	Actual
Main Income		
Extra Income		
Total Income		

Expences:

Category	Budget	Actual
Total		

Sinking funds

Source	Budget	Actual
Total		

Cash Envelopes:

Category	Budget	Actual
Total		

Total Cost to Withdraw: _____

Debt:

Source	Budget	Actual
Total		

Saving

Category	Add	Balance
Total		

	Budget	Actual
Total Funds:		

Monthly Budget Overview

Income

Source	Budget	Actual
Main Income		
Extra Income		
Total Income		

Expences:

Category	Budget	Actual
Total		

Sinking funds

Source	Budget	Actual
Total		

Cash Envelopes:

Category	Budget	Actual
Total		

Total Cost to Withdraw: _____

Debt:

Source	Budget	Actual
Total		

Saving

Category	Add	Balance
Total		

	Budget	Actual
Total Funds:		

Monthly Budget Overview

Income

Source	Budget	Actual
Main Income		
Extra Income		
Total Income		

Expences:

Category	Budget	Actual
Total		

Sinking funds

Source	Budget	Actual
Total		

Cash Envelopes:

Category	Budget	Actual
Total		

Total Cost to Withdraw: _____

Debt:

Source	Budget	Actual
Total		

Saving

Category	Add	Balance
Total		

	Budget	Actual
Total Funds:		

Monthly Budget Overview

Income

Source	Budget	Actual
Main Income		
Extra Income		
Total Income		

Expences:

Category	Budget	Actual
Total		

Sinking funds

Source	Budget	Actual
Total		

Cash Envelopes:

Category	Budget	Actual
Total		

Total Cost to Withdraw: _____

Debt:

Source	Budget	Actual
Total		

Saving

Category	Add	Balance
Total		

	Budget	Actual
Total Funds:		

Monthly Budget Overview

Income

Source	Budget	Actual
Main Income		
Extra Income		
Total Income		

Expences:

Category	Budget	Actual
Total		

Sinking funds

Source	Budget	Actual
Total		

Cash Envelopes:

Category	Budget	Actual
Total		

Total Cost to Withdraw: _____

Debt:

Source	Budget	Actual
Total		

Saving

Category	Add	Balance
Total		

	Budget	Actual
Total Funds:		

Monthly Budget Overview

Income

Source	Budget	Actual
Main Income		
Extra Income		
Total Income		

Expences:

Category	Budget	Actual
Total		

Sinking funds

Source	Budget	Actual
Total		

Cash Envelopes:

Category	Budget	Actual
Total		

Total Cost to Withdraw: _____

Debt:

Source	Budget	Actual
Total		

Saving

Category	Add	Balance
Total		

	Budget	Actual
Total Funds:		

Monthly Budget Overview

Income

Source	Budget	Actual
Main Income		
Extra Income		
Total Income		

Expences:

Category	Budget	Actual
Total		

Sinking funds

Source	Budget	Actual
Total		

Cash Envelopes:

Category	Budget	Actual
Total		

Total Cost to Withdraw: _____

Debt:

Source	Budget	Actual
Total		

Saving

Category	Add	Balance
Total		

	Budget	Actual
Total Funds:		

Monthly Budget Overview

Income

Source	Budget	Actual
Main Income		
Extra Income		
Total Income		

Expences:

Category	Budget	Actual
Total		

Sinking funds

Source	Budget	Actual
Total		

Cash Envelopes:

Category	Budget	Actual
Total		

Total Cost to Withdraw: _____

Debt:

Source	Budget	Actual
Total		

Saving

Category	Add	Balance
Total		

	Budget	Actual
Total Funds:		

Monthly Budget Overview

Income

Source	Budget	Actual
Main Income		
Extra Income		
Total Income		

Expences:

Category	Budget	Actual
Total		

Sinking funds

Source	Budget	Actual
Total		

Cash Envelopes:

Category	Budget	Actual
Total		

Total Cost to Withdraw: _____

Debt:

Source	Budget	Actual
Total		

Saving

Category	Add	Balance
Total		

	Budget	Actual
Total Funds:		

Monthly Budget Overview

Income

Source	Budget	Actual
Main Income		
Extra Income		
Total Income		

Expences:

Category	Budget	Actual
Total		

Sinking funds

Source	Budget	Actual
Total		

Cash Envelopes:

Category	Budget	Actual
Total		

Total Cost to Withdraw: _____

Debt:

Source	Budget	Actual
Total		

Saving

Category	Add	Balance
Total		

	Budget	Actual
Total Funds:		

Monthly Budget Overview

Income

Source	Budget	Actual
Main Income		
Extra Income		
Total Income		

Expences:

Category	Budget	Actual
Total		

Sinking funds

Source	Budget	Actual
Total		

Cash Envelopes:

Category	Budget	Actual
Total		

Total Cost to Withdraw: _____

Debt:

Source	Budget	Actual
Total		

Saving

Category	Add	Balance
Total		

	Budget	Actual
Total Funds:		

Monthly Budget Overview

Income

Source	Budget	Actual
Main Income		
Extra Income		
Total Income		

Expences:

Category	Budget	Actual
Total		

Sinking funds

Source	Budget	Actual
Total		

Cash Envelopes:

Category	Budget	Actual
Total		

Debt:

Source	Budget	Actual
Total		

Saving

Category	Add	Balance
Total		

Total Cost to Withdraw: _____

	Budget	Actual
Total Funds:		

Monthly Budget Overview

Income

Source	Budget	Actual
Main Income		
Extra Income		
Total Income		

Expences:

Category	Budget	Actual
Total		

Sinking funds

Source	Budget	Actual
Total		

Cash Envelopes:

Category	Budget	Actual
Total		

Debt:

Source	Budget	Actual
Total		

Saving

Category	Add	Balance
Total		

Total Cost to Withdraw: _____

	Budget	Actual
Total Funds:		

Monthly Budget Overview

Income

Source	Budget	Actual
Main Income		
Extra Income		
Total Income		

Expences:

Category	Budget	Actual
Total		

Sinking funds

Source	Budget	Actual
Total		

Cash Envelopes:

Category	Budget	Actual
Total		

Debt:

Source	Budget	Actual
Total		

Saving

Category	Add	Balance
Total		

Total Cost to Withdraw: _____

	Budget	Actual
Total Funds:		

Monthly Budget Overview

Income

Source	Budget	Actual
Main Income		
Extra Income		
Total Income		

Expences:

Category	Budget	Actual
Total		

Sinking funds

Source	Budget	Actual
Total		

Cash Envelopes:

Category	Budget	Actual
Total		

Total Cost to Withdraw: _____

Debt:

Source	Budget	Actual
Total		

Saving

Category	Add	Balance
Total		

	Budget	Actual
Total Funds:		

Monthly Budget Overview

Income

Source	Budget	Actual
Main Income		
Extra Income		
Total Income		

Expences:

Category	Budget	Actual
Total		

Sinking funds

Source	Budget	Actual
Total		

Cash Envelopes:

Category	Budget	Actual
Total		

Total Cost to Withdraw: _____

Debt:

Source	Budget	Actual
Total		

Saving

Category	Add	Balance
Total		

	Budget	Actual
Total Funds:		

Monthly Budget Overview

Income

Source	Budget	Actual
Main Income		
Extra Income		
Total Income		

Expences:

Category	Budget	Actual
Total		

Sinking funds

Source	Budget	Actual
Total		

Cash Envelopes:

Category	Budget	Actual
Total		

Total Cost to Withdraw: _____

Debt:

Source	Budget	Actual
Total		

Saving

Category	Add	Balance
Total		

	Budget	Actual
Total Funds:		

Monthly Budget Overview

Income

Source	Budget	Actual
Main Income		
Extra Income		
Total Income		

Expences:

Category	Budget	Actual
Total		

Sinking funds

Source	Budget	Actual
Total		

Cash Envelopes:

Category	Budget	Actual
Total		

Total Cost to Withdraw: _____

Debt:

Source	Budget	Actual
Total		

Saving

Category	Add	Balance
Total		

	Budget	Actual
Total Funds:		

Monthly Budget Overview

Income

Source	Budget	Actual
Main Income		
Extra Income		
Total Income		

Expences:

Category	Budget	Actual
Total		

Sinking funds

Source	Budget	Actual
Total		

Cash Envelopes:

Category	Budget	Actual
Total		

Total Cost to Withdraw: _____

Debt:

Source	Budget	Actual
Total		

Saving

Category	Add	Balance
Total		

	Budget	Actual
Total Funds:		

Monthly Budget Overview

Income

Source	Budget	Actual
Main Income		
Extra Income		
Total Income		

Expences:

Category	Budget	Actual
Total		

Sinking funds

Source	Budget	Actual
Total		

Cash Envelopes:

Category	Budget	Actual
Total		

Total Cost to Withdraw: _____

Debt:

Source	Budget	Actual
Total		

Saving

Category	Add	Balance
Total		

	Budget	Actual
Total Funds:		

Monthly Budget Overview

Income

Source	Budget	Actual
Main Income		
Extra Income		
Total Income		

Expences:

Category	Budget	Actual
Total		

Sinking funds

Source	Budget	Actual
Total		

Cash Envelopes:

Category	Budget	Actual
Total		

Total Cost to Withdraw: _____

Debt:

Source	Budget	Actual
Total		

Saving

Category	Add	Balance
Total		

	Budget	Actual
Total Funds:		

Monthly Budget Overview

Income

Source	Budget	Actual
Main Income		
Extra Income		
Total Income		

Expences:

Category	Budget	Actual
Total		

Sinking funds

Source	Budget	Actual
Total		

Cash Envelopes:

Category	Budget	Actual
Total		

Total Cost to Withdraw: _____

Debt:

Source	Budget	Actual
Total		

Saving

Category	Add	Balance
Total		

	Budget	Actual
Total Funds:		

Monthly Budget Overview

Income

Source	Budget	Actual
Main Income		
Extra Income		
Total Income		

Expences:

Category	Budget	Actual
Total		

Sinking funds

Source	Budget	Actual
Total		

Cash Envelopes:

Category	Budget	Actual
Total		

Total Cost to Withdraw: _____

Debt:

Source	Budget	Actual
Total		

Saving

Category	Add	Balance
Total		

	Budget	Actual
Total Funds:		

Monthly Budget Overview

Income

Source	Budget	Actual
Main Income		
Extra Income		
Total Income		

Expences:

Category	Budget	Actual
Total		

Sinking funds

Source	Budget	Actual
Total		

Cash Envelopes:

Category	Budget	Actual
Total		

Total Cost to Withdraw: _____

Debt:

Source	Budget	Actual
Total		

Saving

Category	Add	Balance
Total		

	Budget	Actual
Total Funds:		

Monthly Budget Overview

Income

Source	Budget	Actual
Main Income		
Extra Income		
Total Income		

Expences:

Category	Budget	Actual
Total		

Sinking funds

Source	Budget	Actual
Total		

Cash Envelopes:

Category	Budget	Actual
Total		

Total Cost to Withdraw: _____

Debt:

Source	Budget	Actual
Total		

Saving

Category	Add	Balance
Total		

	Budget	Actual
Total Funds:		

Monthly Budget Overview

Income

Source	Budget	Actual
Main Income		
Extra Income		
Total Income		

Expences:

Category	Budget	Actual
Total		

Sinking funds

Source	Budget	Actual
Total		

Cash Envelopes:

Category	Budget	Actual
Total		

Total Cost to Withdraw: _____

Debt:

Source	Budget	Actual
Total		

Saving

Category	Add	Balance
Total		

	Budget	Actual
Total Funds:		

Monthly Budget Overview

Income

Source	Budget	Actual
Main Income		
Extra Income		
Total Income		

Expences:

Category	Budget	Actual
Total		

Sinking funds

Source	Budget	Actual
Total		

Cash Envelopes:

Category	Budget	Actual
Total		

Total Cost to Withdraw: _____

Debt:

Source	Budget	Actual
Total		

Saving

Category	Add	Balance
Total		

	Budget	Actual
Total Funds:		

Monthly Budget Overview

Income

Source	Budget	Actual
Main Income		
Extra Income		
Total Income		

Expences:

Category	Budget	Actual
Total		

Sinking funds

Source	Budget	Actual
Total		

Cash Envelopes:

Category	Budget	Actual
Total		

Total Cost to Withdraw: _____

Debt:

Source	Budget	Actual
Total		

Saving

Category	Add	Balance
Total		

	Budget	Actual
Total Funds:		

Monthly Budget Overview

Income

Source	Budget	Actual
Main Income		
Extra Income		
Total Income		

Expences:

Category	Budget	Actual
Total		

Sinking funds

Source	Budget	Actual
Total		

Cash Envelopes:

Category	Budget	Actual
Total		

Total Cost to Withdraw: _____

Debt:

Source	Budget	Actual
Total		

Saving

Category	Add	Balance
Total		

	Budget	Actual
Total Funds:		

Monthly Budget Overview

Income

Source	Budget	Actual
Main Income		
Extra Income		
Total Income		

Expences:

Category	Budget	Actual
Total		

Sinking funds

Source	Budget	Actual
Total		

Cash Envelopes:

Category	Budget	Actual
Total		

Total Cost to Withdraw: _____

Debt:

Source	Budget	Actual
Total		

Saving

Category	Add	Balance
Total		

	Budget	Actual
Total Funds:		

Monthly Budget Overview

Income

Source	Budget	Actual
Main Income		
Extra Income		
Total Income		

Expences:

Category	Budget	Actual
Total		

Sinking funds

Source	Budget	Actual
Total		

Cash Envelopes:

Category	Budget	Actual
Total		

Total Cost to Withdraw: _____

Debt:

Source	Budget	Actual
Total		

Saving

Category	Add	Balance
Total		

	Budget	Actual
Total Funds:		

Monthly Budget Overview

Income

Source	Budget	Actual
Main Income		
Extra Income		
Total Income		

Expences:

Category	Budget	Actual
Total		

Sinking funds

Source	Budget	Actual
Total		

Cash Envelopes:

Category	Budget	Actual
Total		

Total Cost to Withdraw: _____

Debt:

Source	Budget	Actual
Total		

Saving

Category	Add	Balance
Total		

	Budget	Actual
Total Funds:		

Monthly Budget Overview

Income

Source	Budget	Actual
Main Income		
Extra Income		
Total Income		

Expences:

Category	Budget	Actual
Total		

Sinking funds

Source	Budget	Actual
Total		

Cash Envelopes:

Category	Budget	Actual
Total		

Total Cost to Withdraw: _____

Debt:

Source	Budget	Actual
Total		

Saving

Category	Add	Balance
Total		

	Budget	Actual
Total Funds:		

Monthly Budget Overview

Income

Source	Budget	Actual
Main Income		
Extra Income		
Total Income		

Expences:

Category	Budget	Actual
Total		

Sinking funds

Source	Budget	Actual
Total		

Cash Envelopes:

Category	Budget	Actual
Total		

Total Cost to Withdraw: _____

Debt:

Source	Budget	Actual
Total		

Saving

Category	Add	Balance
Total		

	Budget	Actual
Total Funds:		

Monthly Budget Overview

Income

Source	Budget	Actual
Main Income		
Extra Income		
Total Income		

Expences:

Category	Budget	Actual
Total		

Sinking funds

Source	Budget	Actual
Total		

Cash Envelopes:

Category	Budget	Actual
Total		

Total Cost to Withdraw: _____

Debt:

Source	Budget	Actual
Total		

Saving

Category	Add	Balance
Total		

	Budget	Actual
Total Funds:		

Monthly Budget Overview

Income

Source	Budget	Actual
Main Income		
Extra Income		
Total Income		

Expences:

Category	Budget	Actual
Total		

Sinking funds

Source	Budget	Actual
Total		

Cash Envelopes:

Category	Budget	Actual
Total		

Debt:

Source	Budget	Actual
Total		

Saving

Category	Add	Balance
Total		

Total Cost to Withdraw: _____

	Budget	Actual
Total Funds:		

Monthly Budget Overview

Income

Source	Budget	Actual
Main Income		
Extra Income		
Total Income		

Expences:

Category	Budget	Actual
Total		

Sinking funds

Source	Budget	Actual
Total		

Cash Envelopes:

Category	Budget	Actual
Total		

Total Cost to Withdraw: _____

Debt:

Source	Budget	Actual
Total		

Saving

Category	Add	Balance
Total		

	Budget	Actual
Total Funds:		

Monthly Budget Overview

Income

Source	Budget	Actual
Main Income		
Extra Income		
Total Income		

Expences:

Category	Budget	Actual
Total		

Sinking funds

Source	Budget	Actual
Total		

Cash Envelopes:

Category	Budget	Actual
Total		

Total Cost to Withdraw: _____

Debt:

Source	Budget	Actual
Total		

Saving

Category	Add	Balance
Total		

	Budget	Actual
Total Funds:		

Monthly Budget Overview

Income

Source	Budget	Actual
Main Income		
Extra Income		
Total Income		

Expences:

Category	Budget	Actual
Total		

Sinking funds

Source	Budget	Actual
Total		

Cash Envelopes:

Category	Budget	Actual
Total		

Debt:

Source	Budget	Actual
Total		

Saving

Category	Add	Balance
Total		

Total Cost to Withdraw: _____

	Budget	Actual
Total Funds:		

Monthly Budget Overview

Income

Source	Budget	Actual
Main Income		
Extra Income		
Total Income		

Expences:

Category	Budget	Actual
Total		

Sinking funds

Source	Budget	Actual
Total		

Cash Envelopes:

Category	Budget	Actual
Total		

Total Cost to Withdraw: _____

Debt:

Source	Budget	Actual
Total		

Saving

Category	Add	Balance
Total		

	Budget	Actual
Total Funds:		

Monthly Budget Overview

Income

Source	Budget	Actual
Main Income		
Extra Income		
Total Income		

Expences:

Category	Budget	Actual
Total		

Sinking funds

Source	Budget	Actual
Total		

Cash Envelopes:

Category	Budget	Actual
Total		

Total Cost to Withdraw: _____

Debt:

Source	Budget	Actual
Total		

Saving

Category	Add	Balance
Total		

	Budget	Actual
Total Funds:		

Monthly Budget Overview

Income

Source	Budget	Actual
Main Income		
Extra Income		
Total Income		

Expences:

Category	Budget	Actual
Total		

Sinking funds

Source	Budget	Actual
Total		

Cash Envelopes:

Category	Budget	Actual
Total		

Total Cost to Withdraw: _____

Debt:

Source	Budget	Actual
Total		

Saving

Category	Add	Balance
Total		

	Budget	Actual
Total Funds:		

Monthly Budget Overview

Income

Source	Budget	Actual
Main Income		
Extra Income		
Total Income		

Expences:

Category	Budget	Actual
Total		

Sinking funds

Source	Budget	Actual
Total		

Cash Envelopes:

Category	Budget	Actual
Total		

Total Cost to Withdraw: _____

Debt:

Source	Budget	Actual
Total		

Saving

Category	Add	Balance
Total		

	Budget	Actual
Total Funds:		

Monthly Budget Overview

Income

Source	Budget	Actual
Main Income		
Extra Income		
Total Income		

Expences:

Category	Budget	Actual
Total		

Sinking funds

Source	Budget	Actual
Total		

Cash Envelopes:

Category	Budget	Actual
Total		

Total Cost to Withdraw: _____

Debt:

Source	Budget	Actual
Total		

Saving

Category	Add	Balance
Total		

	Budget	Actual
Total Funds:		

Monthly Budget Overview

Income

Source	Budget	Actual
Main Income		
Extra Income		
Total Income		

Expences:

Category	Budget	Actual
Total		

Sinking funds

Source	Budget	Actual
Total		

Cash Envelopes:

Category	Budget	Actual
Total		

Total Cost to Withdraw: _____

Debt:

Source	Budget	Actual
Total		

Saving

Category	Add	Balance
Total		

	Budget	Actual
Total Funds:		

Monthly Budget Overview

Income

Source	Budget	Actual
Main Income		
Extra Income		
Total Income		

Expences:

Category	Budget	Actual
Total		

Sinking funds

Source	Budget	Actual
Total		

Cash Envelopes:

Category	Budget	Actual
Total		

Total Cost to Withdraw: _____

Debt:

Source	Budget	Actual
Total		

Saving

Category	Add	Balance
Total		

	Budget	Actual
Total Funds:		

Monthly Budget Overview

Income

Source	Budget	Actual
Main Income		
Extra Income		
Total Income		

Expences:

Category	Budget	Actual
Total		

Sinking funds

Source	Budget	Actual
Total		

Cash Envelopes:

Category	Budget	Actual
Total		

Total Cost to Withdraw: _____

Debt:

Source	Budget	Actual
Total		

Saving

Category	Add	Balance
Total		

	Budget	Actual
Total Funds:		

Monthly Budget Overview

Income

Source	Budget	Actual
Main Income		
Extra Income		
Total Income		

Expences:

Category	Budget	Actual
Total		

Sinking funds

Source	Budget	Actual
Total		

Cash Envelopes:

Category	Budget	Actual
Total		

Debt:

Source	Budget	Actual
Total		

Saving

Category	Add	Balance
Total		

Total Cost to Withdraw: _____

	Budget	Actual
Total Funds:		

Monthly Budget Overview

Income

Source	Budget	Actual
Main Income		
Extra Income		
Total Income		

Expences:

Category	Budget	Actual
Total		

Sinking funds

Source	Budget	Actual
Total		

Cash Envelopes:

Category	Budget	Actual
Total		

Total Cost to Withdraw: _____

Debt:

Source	Budget	Actual
Total		

Saving

Category	Add	Balance
Total		

	Budget	Actual
Total Funds:		

Monthly Budget Overview

Income

Source	Budget	Actual
Main Income		
Extra Income		
Total Income		

Expences:

Category	Budget	Actual
Total		

Sinking funds

Source	Budget	Actual
Total		

Cash Envelopes:

Category	Budget	Actual
Total		

Total Cost to Withdraw: _____

Debt:

Source	Budget	Actual
Total		

Saving

Category	Add	Balance
Total		

	Budget	Actual
Total Funds:		

Monthly Budget Overview

Income

Source	Budget	Actual
Main Income		
Extra Income		
Total Income		

Expences:

Category	Budget	Actual
Total		

Sinking funds

Source	Budget	Actual
Total		

Cash Envelopes:

Category	Budget	Actual
Total		

Total Cost to Withdraw: _____

Debt:

Source	Budget	Actual
Total		

Saving

Category	Add	Balance
Total		

	Budget	Actual
Total Funds:		

Monthly Budget Overview

Income

Source	Budget	Actual
Main Income		
Extra Income		
Total Income		

Expences:

Category	Budget	Actual
Total		

Sinking funds

Source	Budget	Actual
Total		

Cash Envelopes:

Category	Budget	Actual
Total		

Total Cost to Withdraw: _____

Debt:

Source	Budget	Actual
Total		

Saving

Category	Add	Balance
Total		

	Budget	Actual
Total Funds:		

Monthly Budget Overview

Income

Source	Budget	Actual
Main Income		
Extra Income		
Total Income		

Expences:

Category	Budget	Actual
Total		

Sinking funds

Source	Budget	Actual
Total		

Cash Envelopes:

Category	Budget	Actual
Total		

Total Cost to Withdraw: _____

Debt:

Source	Budget	Actual
Total		

Saving

Category	Add	Balance
Total		

	Budget	Actual
Total Funds:		

Monthly Budget Overview

Income

Source	Budget	Actual
Main Income		
Extra Income		
Total Income		

Expences:

Category	Budget	Actual
Total		

Sinking funds

Source	Budget	Actual
Total		

Cash Envelopes:

Category	Budget	Actual
Total		

Total Cost to Withdraw: _____

Debt:

Source	Budget	Actual
Total		

Saving

Category	Add	Balance
Total		

	Budget	Actual
Total Funds:		

Monthly Budget Overview

Income

Source	Budget	Actual
Main Income		
Extra Income		
Total Income		

Expences:

Category	Budget	Actual
Total		

Sinking funds

Source	Budget	Actual
Total		

Cash Envelopes:

Category	Budget	Actual
Total		

Debt:

Source	Budget	Actual
Total		

Saving

Category	Add	Balance
Total		

Total Cost to Withdraw: _____

	Budget	Actual
Total Funds:		

Monthly Budget Overview

Income

Source	Budget	Actual
Main Income		
Extra Income		
Total Income		

Expences:

Category	Budget	Actual
Total		

Sinking funds

Source	Budget	Actual
Total		

Cash Envelopes:

Category	Budget	Actual
Total		

Total Cost to Withdraw: _____

Debt:

Source	Budget	Actual
Total		

Saving

Category	Add	Balance
Total		

	Budget	Actual
Total Funds:		

Monthly Budget Overview

Income

Source	Budget	Actual
Main Income		
Extra Income		
Total Income		

Expences:

Category	Budget	Actual
Total		

Sinking funds

Source	Budget	Actual
Total		

Cash Envelopes:

Category	Budget	Actual
Total		

Debt:

Source	Budget	Actual
Total		

Saving

Category	Add	Balance
Total		

Total Cost to Withdraw: _____

	Budget	Actual
Total Funds:		

Monthly Budget Overview

Income

Source	Budget	Actual
Main Income		
Extra Income		
Total Income		

Expences:

Category	Budget	Actual
Total		

Sinking funds

Source	Budget	Actual
Total		

Cash Envelopes:

Category	Budget	Actual
Total		

Total Cost to Withdraw: _____

Debt:

Source	Budget	Actual
Total		

Saving

Category	Add	Balance
Total		

	Budget	Actual
Total Funds:		

Monthly Budget Overview

Income

Source	Budget	Actual
Main Income		
Extra Income		
Total Income		

Expences:

Category	Budget	Actual
Total		

Sinking funds

Source	Budget	Actual
Total		

Cash Envelopes:

Category	Budget	Actual
Total		

Total Cost to Withdraw: _____

Debt:

Source	Budget	Actual
Total		

Saving

Category	Add	Balance
Total		

	Budget	Actual
Total Funds:		

Monthly Budget Overview

Income

Source	Budget	Actual
Main Income		
Extra Income		
Total Income		

Expences:

Category	Budget	Actual
Total		

Sinking funds

Source	Budget	Actual
Total		

Cash Envelopes:

Category	Budget	Actual
Total		

Total Cost to Withdraw: _____

Debt:

Source	Budget	Actual
Total		

Saving

Category	Add	Balance
Total		

	Budget	Actual
Total Funds:		

Monthly Budget Overview

Income

Source	Budget	Actual
Main Income		
Extra Income		
Total Income		

Expences:

Category	Budget	Actual
Total		

Sinking funds

Source	Budget	Actual
Total		

Cash Envelopes:

Category	Budget	Actual
Total		

Total Cost to Withdraw: _____

Debt:

Source	Budget	Actual
Total		

Saving

Category	Add	Balance
Total		

	Budget	Actual
Total Funds:		

Monthly Budget Overview

Income

Source	Budget	Actual
Main Income		
Extra Income		
Total Income		

Expences:

Category	Budget	Actual
Total		

Sinking funds

Source	Budget	Actual
Total		

Cash Envelopes:

Category	Budget	Actual
Total		

Total Cost to Withdraw: _____

Debt:

Source	Budget	Actual
Total		

Saving

Category	Add	Balance
Total		

	Budget	Actual
Total Funds:		

Monthly Budget Overview

Income

Source	Budget	Actual
Main Income		
Extra Income		
Total Income		

Expences:

Category	Budget	Actual
Total		

Sinking funds

Source	Budget	Actual
Total		

Cash Envelopes:

Category	Budget	Actual
Total		

Total Cost to Withdraw: _____

Debt:

Source	Budget	Actual
Total		

Saving

Category	Add	Balance
Total		

	Budget	Actual
Total Funds:		

Monthly Budget Overview

Income

Source	Budget	Actual
Main Income		
Extra Income		
Total Income		

Expences:

Category	Budget	Actual
Total		

Sinking funds

Source	Budget	Actual
Total		

Cash Envelopes:

Category	Budget	Actual
Total		

Debt:

Source	Budget	Actual
Total		

Saving

Category	Add	Balance
Total		

Total Cost to Withdraw: _____

	Budget	Actual
Total Funds:		

Monthly Budget Overview

Income

Source	Budget	Actual
Main Income		
Extra Income		
Total Income		

Expences:

Category	Budget	Actual
Total		

Sinking funds

Source	Budget	Actual
Total		

Cash Envelopes:

Category	Budget	Actual
Total		

Total Cost to Withdraw: _____

Debt:

Source	Budget	Actual
Total		

Saving

Category	Add	Balance
Total		

	Budget	Actual
Total Funds:		

Monthly Budget Overview

Income

Source	Budget	Actual
Main Income		
Extra Income		
Total Income		

Expences:

Category	Budget	Actual
Total		

Sinking funds

Source	Budget	Actual
Total		

Cash Envelopes:

Category	Budget	Actual
Total		

Total Cost to Withdraw: _____

Debt:

Source	Budget	Actual
Total		

Saving

Category	Add	Balance
Total		

	Budget	Actual
Total Funds:		

Monthly Budget Overview

Income

Source	Budget	Actual
Main Income		
Extra Income		
Total Income		

Expences:

Category	Budget	Actual
Total		

Sinking funds

Source	Budget	Actual
Total		

Cash Envelopes:

Category	Budget	Actual
Total		

Debt:

Source	Budget	Actual
Total		

Saving

Category	Add	Balance
Total		

Total Cost to Withdraw: _____

	Budget	Actual
Total Funds:		

Monthly Budget Overview

Income

Source	Budget	Actual
Main Income		
Extra Income		
Total Income		

Expences:

Category	Budget	Actual
Total		

Sinking funds

Source	Budget	Actual
Total		

Cash Envelopes:

Category	Budget	Actual
Total		

Total Cost to Withdraw: _____

Debt:

Source	Budget	Actual
Total		

Saving

Category	Add	Balance
Total		

	Budget	Actual
Total Funds:		

Monthly Budget Overview

Income

Source	Budget	Actual
Main Income		
Extra Income		
Total Income		

Expences:

Category	Budget	Actual
Total		

Sinking funds

Source	Budget	Actual
Total		

Cash Envelopes:

Category	Budget	Actual
Total		

Total Cost to Withdraw: _____

Debt:

Source	Budget	Actual
Total		

Saving

Category	Add	Balance
Total		

	Budget	Actual
Total Funds:		

Monthly Budget Overview

Income

Source	Budget	Actual
Main Income		
Extra Income		
Total Income		

Expences:

Category	Budget	Actual
Total		

Sinking funds

Source	Budget	Actual
Total		

Cash Envelopes:

Category	Budget	Actual
Total		

Total Cost to Withdraw: _____

Debt:

Source	Budget	Actual
Total		

Saving

Category	Add	Balance
Total		

	Budget	Actual
Total Funds:		

Monthly Budget Overview

Income

Source	Budget	Actual
Main Income		
Extra Income		
Total Income		

Expences:

Category	Budget	Actual
Total		

Sinking funds

Source	Budget	Actual
Total		

Cash Envelopes:

Category	Budget	Actual
Total		

Debt:

Source	Budget	Actual
Total		

Saving

Category	Add	Balance
Total		

Total Cost to Withdraw: _____

	Budget	Actual
Total Funds:		

Monthly Budget Overview

Income

Source	Budget	Actual
Main Income		
Extra Income		
Total Income		

Expences:

Category	Budget	Actual
Total		

Sinking funds

Source	Budget	Actual
Total		

Cash Envelopes:

Category	Budget	Actual
Total		

Debt:

Source	Budget	Actual
Total		

Saving

Category	Add	Balance
Total		

Total Cost to Withdraw: _____

	Budget	Actual
Total Funds:		

Monthly Budget Overview

Income

Source	Budget	Actual
Main Income		
Extra Income		
Total Income		

Expences:

Category	Budget	Actual
Total		

Sinking funds

Source	Budget	Actual
Total		

Cash Envelopes:

Category	Budget	Actual
Total		

Total Cost to Withdraw: _____

Debt:

Source	Budget	Actual
Total		

Saving

Category	Add	Balance
Total		

	Budget	Actual
Total Funds:		

Monthly Budget Overview

Income

Source	Budget	Actual
Main Income		
Extra Income		
Total Income		

Expences:

Category	Budget	Actual
Total		

Sinking funds

Source	Budget	Actual
Total		

Cash Envelopes:

Category	Budget	Actual
Total		

Total Cost to Withdraw: _____

Debt:

Source	Budget	Actual
Total		

Saving

Category	Add	Balance
Total		

	Budget	Actual
Total Funds:		

Monthly Budget Overview

Income

Source	Budget	Actual
Main Income		
Extra Income		
Total Income		

Expences:

Category	Budget	Actual
Total		

Sinking funds

Source	Budget	Actual
Total		

Cash Envelopes:

Category	Budget	Actual
Total		

Total Cost to Withdraw: _____

Debt:

Source	Budget	Actual
Total		

Saving

Category	Add	Balance
Total		

	Budget	Actual
Total Funds:		

Monthly Budget Overview

Income

Source	Budget	Actual
Main Income		
Extra Income		
Total Income		

Expences:

Category	Budget	Actual
Total		

Sinking funds

Source	Budget	Actual
Total		

Cash Envelopes:

Category	Budget	Actual
Total		

Total Cost to Withdraw: _____

Debt:

Source	Budget	Actual
Total		

Saving

Category	Add	Balance
Total		

	Budget	Actual
Total Funds:		

Monthly Budget Overview

Income

Source	Budget	Actual
Main Income		
Extra Income		
Total Income		

Expences:

Category	Budget	Actual
Total		

Sinking funds

Source	Budget	Actual
Total		

Cash Envelopes:

Category	Budget	Actual
Total		

Total Cost to Withdraw: _____

Debt:

Source	Budget	Actual
Total		

Saving

Category	Add	Balance
Total		

	Budget	Actual
Total Funds:		

Monthly Budget Overview

Income

Source	Budget	Actual
Main Income		
Extra Income		
Total Income		

Expences:

Category	Budget	Actual
Total		

Sinking funds

Source	Budget	Actual
Total		

Cash Envelopes:

Category	Budget	Actual
Total		

Total Cost to Withdraw: _____

Debt:

Source	Budget	Actual
Total		

Saving

Category	Add	Balance
Total		

	Budget	Actual
Total Funds:		

Monthly Budget Overview

Income

Source	Budget	Actual
Main Income		
Extra Income		
Total Income		

Expences:

Category	Budget	Actual
Total		

Sinking funds

Source	Budget	Actual
Total		

Cash Envelopes:

Category	Budget	Actual
Total		

Total Cost to Withdraw: _____

Debt:

Source	Budget	Actual
Total		

Saving

Category	Add	Balance
Total		

	Budget	Actual
Total Funds:		

Monthly Budget Overview

Income

Source	Budget	Actual
Main Income		
Extra Income		
Total Income		

Expences:

Category	Budget	Actual
Total		

Sinking funds

Source	Budget	Actual
Total		

Cash Envelopes:

Category	Budget	Actual
Total		

Total Cost to Withdraw: _____

Debt:

Source	Budget	Actual
Total		

Saving

Category	Add	Balance
Total		

	Budget	Actual
Total Funds:		

Monthly Budget Overview

Income

Source	Budget	Actual
Main Income		
Extra Income		
Total Income		

Expences:

Category	Budget	Actual
Total		

Sinking funds

Source	Budget	Actual
Total		

Cash Envelopes:

Category	Budget	Actual
Total		

Total Cost to Withdraw: _____

Debt:

Source	Budget	Actual
Total		

Saving

Category	Add	Balance
Total		

	Budget	Actual
Total Funds:		

Monthly Budget Overview

Income

Source	Budget	Actual
Main Income		
Extra Income		
Total Income		

Expences:

Category	Budget	Actual
Total		

Sinking funds

Source	Budget	Actual
Total		

Cash Envelopes:

Category	Budget	Actual
Total		

Total Cost to Withdraw: _____

Debt:

Source	Budget	Actual
Total		

Saving

Category	Add	Balance
Total		

	Budget	Actual
Total Funds:		

www.ingramcontent.com/pod-product-compliance
Lightning Source LLC
Chambersburg PA
CBHW070802040426
42333CB00061B/1768